高等学校英语类"十三五"规划教材

新媒体时代跨文化交际
视听说教程

主　编　陈争峰

副主编　杨延红　郑　沛　赵　蓉　孟广兰

西安电子科技大学出版社

内 容 简 介

  本书以英美国家地道的英语影视片段、音频和相关的交际案例等视听素材为载体,通过案例,对文化、交际、语言、跨文化交际等相关知识进行描述和阐释,目的是增强大学生的跨文化交际意识。全书分为 8 章,每一章都围绕英美跨文化交际的主题展开,附有听力理解习题和口语的讨论、辩论训练。第一章介绍跨文化交际的知识背景;第二章介绍语言和文化的多样性;第三章讲述文化的价值观,文化的休克与适应以及文化的准则;第四章讲述跨文化的洞察力意识;第五章讨论了跨文化交际的语境;第六章阐述了跨文化适应过程中的障碍;第七章讲述英美国家的文化标记和文化象征;两个附录分别是音、视频参考文本及每章的课后题答案。本书以跨文化交际为切入点,以英语听说为主干,采用多媒体技术,融合视频和音频的多模态表现手法,把英美文化知识的渗透作为重点,注重跨文化知识的传递和文化意识的培养,并结合最新的四、六级听力实战模拟题(2018、2019 新题型),做到学与练的有机结合,提高学生跨文化交际的意识和能力。

图书在版编目(CIP)数据

新媒体时代跨文化交际视听说教程 / 陈争峰主编. —西安:西安电子科技大学出版社,2018.9
ISBN 978-7-5606-5038-8

Ⅰ. ① 新… Ⅱ. ① 陈… Ⅲ. ① 英语—听说教学—高等学校—教材 Ⅳ. ① H319.9

中国版本图书馆 CIP 数据核字(2018)第 181389 号

策划编辑 刘小莉
责任编辑 卢 杨 阎 彬
出版发行 西安电子科技大学出版社(西安市太白南路 2 号)
电 话 (029)88242885 88201467   邮 编 710071
网 址 www.xduph.com   电子邮箱 xdupfxb001@163.com
经 销 新华书店
印刷单位 陕西天意印务有限责任公司
版 次 2018 年 9 月第 1 版 2018 年 9 月第 1 次印刷
开 本 787 毫米×1092 毫米 1/16 印 张 11.5
字 数 268 千字
印 数 1～2000 册
定 价 25.00 元

ISBN 978-7-5606-5038-8 / H

XDUP 5340001-1

如有印装问题可调换

前　　言

随着全球化进程的深入，中国与世界的跨文化交际也日显重要，这就要求非英语专业的本科生，尤其是理工科专业的学生，不但要学好作为交际工具使用的英语语言，还要具有很强的跨文化视听说交际能力。依据教育部颁布的教学大纲的要求，基于多年来在大学英语教学方面的探索及对学生实际需求的了解，尤其是针对非英语专业大学生英语听说能力薄弱和跨文化交际能力不强这一现状，我们课题组结合四、六级最新题型的新发展趋势，编写了本书。

该书适应当前本科生"国际化"教育教学改革发展的需要，着眼于中西文化交际，以影视片段、相关文章和交际案例等视听素材为载体，通过案例对文化、交际、语言、跨文化交际等相关知识进行描述和阐释，通过视、听、说，以及师生之间、生生之间的口语交互活动来促进学生对跨文化的理解，增强学生的跨文化意识。本书的编写突出大学生交际能力培养，每一章都附有听力理解习题（复合式听写、篇章理解和对话理解）、口语讨论和辩论训练，以便加深学生对跨文化交际中有关问题的理解与认识，并借此检验学生的听说能力。本书对考试具有指导性和实战性，它是大学生参加英语考试的好帮手，同时也是培养学生成为国际复合型专业人才的必备教材。本书的音频和视频资料链接地址为：https://pan.baidu.com/s/1frjiaSWiK1SzoybwO80eLg 密码：3u9c；或 https://pan.baidu.com/s/1i0QzbI4e9j4yO9oaQWTw6Q 密码：ou37。

本书可作为高校英语专业本科生的基础课教材、高等院校非英语专业本科生公共选修课的教材，也可作为大学生四、六级考试的听说教材，亦可供对英美国家文化感兴趣的学者参考。

我们课题组希望通过本书，能够进一步增进学生对英美国家文化的了解，拓宽他们的国际文化视野，进一步提高他们的英语跨文化交际听说能力。

本书的编写得到了西安电子科技大学教材基金(BJ1518)的资助；获得了

2017 年陕西省教育科学规划课题(SGH17H050)：后 MOOC 时代下 O2O 大学英语教学模式构建研究以及西安市社科基金项目(17Y27)：国际化背景下西安高校英语教学中文化自信观的构建研究的资助；还获得了 2017 年中央高校基本科研业务费专项资金重点资助项目 RW170403 和一般资助项目 RW170116 的资助。编者在此表示衷心的感谢！同时也感谢西安电子科技大学出版社的大力支持及编辑刘小莉的悉心指导和帮助！

在此，还要感谢我的同事杨延红、赵蓉、孟广兰、郑沛等，她们辛勤和认真的付出，保证了本书编写工作的有序进行。与此同时，也要感谢我的学生们，感谢他们对课堂教学信息的及时反馈和对教学工作的积极支持与配合。

本书所引用的材料一般已注明出处或列在参考文献中，没有注明出处的是由于辗转引用，未能查出原作者和出处，编者在此一并表示衷心的感谢！

由于水平有限，书中难免存在不足之处，恳请广大读者给予批评指正。

陈争峰

2018 年 4 月

于西安电子科技大学外国语学院

Contents

Chapter 1   Intercultural Communication

1.1   Intercultural Background

1.1.1   Definition of the Interculture

The multicultural world is enhanced by the experiences of sojourners, merchants, immigrants, and others that successfully transitioned from one culture to another. The individual becomes more mature and knowledgeable. The world becomes more diverse and at the same time becomes more understanding. A variety of perspectives on acculturation and the concept of intercultural identity are discussed, with research support and related communication theories highlighted. This overview of acculturation and intercultural identity presents the most current research in the area with suggestions for future investigations.

Intercultural communication is a form of communication that aims to share information across different cultures and social groups. It is used to describe the wide range of communication processes and problems that naturally appear within an organization or social context made up of individuals from different religious, social, ethnic, and educational backgrounds. Intercultural communication is sometimes used synonymously with cross-cultural communication.

In this sense it seeks to understand how people from different countries and cultures act, communicate and perceive the world around them. Many people in intercultural business communication argue that culture determines how individuals encode messages, what medium they choose for transmitting them, and the way messages are interpreted. With regard to intercultural communication correctness, it studies situations where people from different cultural backgrounds interact. Aside from language, intercultural communication focuses on social attributes, thought patterns, and the cultures of different groups of people. It also involves understanding the different cultures, languages and customs of people from other countries. Intercultural communication plays a role in social sciences such as anthropology, cultural studies, linguistics, psychology and communication studies.

1.1.2   Features of Intercultural Communication

Cultural identity is the identity or feeling of belonging to a group. It is a part of a person's self-conception and self-perception and is related to nationality, ethnicity, religion, social class, generation, locality or any kind of social group that has its own distinct culture. In this way, cultural identity is both characteristic of the individual but also of the culturally identical group of members sharing the same cultural identity. Modern culture is essential to our understanding of ourselves and our universe. Various modern cultural studies and social theories have investigated cultural identity. In recent decades, a new form of identification has emerged which breaks down the understanding of the individual as a coherent whole subject into a collection of various cultural identifiers. These cultural identifiers may be the result of various conditions including: location, gender, race, history, nationality, language, sexuality, religious beliefs, ethnicity, aesthetics, and even food. As one author writes, recognizing both coherence and fragmentation, "categorizations about identity, even when codified and hardened into clear typologies by processes of colonization, state formation or general modernizing processes, are always full of tensions and contradictions. Sometimes these contradictions are destructive, but they can also be creative and positive."

Intercultural identity is used to identify an individual's ability to grow beyond their original culture and encompass a new culture, gaining additional insight into both cultures in the process. These theories of acculturation and intercultural identity describe communication as the mediating process required to facilitate the transition from one culture to the next. "Communication is crucial to acculturation. It provides the fundamental means by which individuals develop insights into their new environment." This means that increasing interpersonal communication within the new host environment will result in increased acculturation. Interpersonal communication with those residents of the new host culture is expected to facilitate acculturation. In order to accomplish interpersonal communication within the indigenous resident community of the new host culture, language competence is necessary. In a similar way, language competence is also required to fully utilize the host culture's mass media. Therefore increased language competence will increase both interpersonal communication and mass media usage. This vision of the intercultural identity acculturation process provides a vision of the future worthy of aspiration. Cultures are valued and maintained for their inherent value as well as their value of diversity to the world. The ability to build cultures within cultures, and communicate effectively on an inter-ethnic, an intercultural and an international level will most likely be necessary for almost everyone.

1.2　The Features of Contemporary World Culture

1.2.1　Constant Change

No matter what culture the people are a part of, one thing is for certain—it will change. Culture appears to have become key in our interconnected world, which is made up of so many ethnically diverse societies, but also riddled by conflicts associated with religion, ethnicity, ethical beliefs, and, essentially, the elements which make up culture. De Rossi said: "But culture is no longer fixed, if it ever was. It is essentially fluid and constantly in motion." This makes it so that it is difficult to define any culture in only one way.

1.2.2　Cultural Diversity

Culture is the characteristics and knowledge of a particular group of people, defined by everything from language, religion, cuisine, social habits, music and arts. The Center for Advance Research on Language Acquisition goes a step further, defining culture as shared patterns of behaviors and interactions, cognitive constructs and understanding that are learned by socialization. Thus, it can be seen as the growth of a group identity fostered by social patterns unique to the group. Many countries are largely populated by immigrants, and the culture is influenced by the many groups of people that now make up the country. This is also a part of growth. As the countries grow, so does its cultural diversity. The multicultural world is enhanced by the experiences of different people and transited from one culture to another. The individual becomes more mature and knowledgeable. The world becomes more diverse and at the same time becomes more understanding.

Culture, the total way of life that characterizes a group of people, is one of the most important things for communication. There are literally thousands of cultures on Earth today, and each contributes to global diversity. One reason for the existence of so many cultures is that there are so many ways that people all over the world can be culturally different. Specifically, a culture consists of numerous cultural components—religion, language, architecture, cuisine, technology, music, dance, sports, medicine, dress, gender roles, law, education government, agriculture，economy，grooming, values, work ethic, etiquette , courtship, recreation , gestures, which varies from one culture group to the next. For example, language is a cultural component. While some cultural communities use English, others speak Spanish, Japanese, Arabic, or another of the thousands of languages spoken today. Religion is another cultural component, and there are hundreds (if not thousands) of ways that different culture groups practice and are characterized by that trait.

1.3　Pre-watching Activities

Video One：Leonardo's Speech

★　New Words

endeavor 努力	nominee 被提名的人
transcendent 跨越，超越	procrastinate 推迟，拖延
humanity 人文性	indigenous 聪明
underprivileged 被剥夺权利的	

1.3.1　Compound Dictation One

Thank you all so very much. Thank you to the Academy, thank you to all of you in this room. I have to congratulate the other _____1_____ nominees this year for their _____2_____. The Revenant was the product of the tireless efforts of an unbelievable cast and crew I got to work alongside. First off, to my brother in this endeavor, Mr.Tom Hardy. Tom, your _____3_____ on screen can only be surpassed by your friendship off screen. To Mr. Alejandro Innaritu, as the history of cinema unfolds, _____4_____ thank you for creating a transcendent cinematic experience. Thank you to everybody at Fox and New Regency...my entire team. I have to thank everyone from the very onset of my career...to Mr. Jones for casting me in my first film to Mr. Scorsese for teaching me so much about the cinematic art form. To my parents, none of this would be possible without you. And to my friends, I love you dearly, you know who you are.

And lastly I just want to say this: making The Revenant was about man's relationship to the natural world. A world that we _____5_____ felt in 2015 as the hottest year in recorded history. Our production needed to move to the southern tip of this planet just to be able to find snow. _____6_____, it is happening right now. _____7_____, and we need to work collectively together and stop procrastinating.

We need to support leaders around the world who do not speak for the _____8_____, but who speak for all of humanity, for the indigenous people of the world, for the billions and billions of underprivileged people out there who would be most affected by this. For our children's children, and for those people out there whose voices have been drowned out by the politics of greed. I thank you all for _____9_____. Let us not take this planet for granted. I do not _____10_____. Thank you so very much.

1.3.2　Conversation Practice

1. What is your understanding of Leonardo's success in winning the Oscar Award? Why does he achieve the success?

2. Who is the biggest polluter in this world? Who should be blamed for the deterioration of the environment? As for human species what shall we do for the environmental protection?

1.4　Watching Activities

Video Two: Photos that Changed the World

★　**New Words**

naive 简单的，幼稚的	photography 图片

iconic 讽刺的	uncompromising 不妥协的
crucial 重要的	crucifixion 屠杀
outrage 愤怒	profound 深刻
cemetery 坟墓	relief 减轻

1.4.1   Compound Dictation Two

In my industry, we believe that images can change the world. Okay, we're naive, we're bright-eyed and bushy-tailed. The truth is that we know that the images themselves don't change the world, but we're also aware that, since the beginning of photography,＿＿＿＿＿＿＿＿＿＿

＿＿＿＿＿＿＿＿＿＿＿＿＿＿1＿＿＿＿＿＿＿＿＿＿＿＿＿＿．

So let's begin with a group of images. I'd be extremely surprised if you didn't recognize many or most of them. They're best described as iconic, so iconic, perhaps they're cliches. In fact, they're so well-known that you might even recognize them in a   slightly or somewhat different form.

But I think we're looking for something more. We're looking for something more. We're looking for images that shine an uncompromising light on crucial issues, ＿＿＿＿＿＿＿＿＿

＿＿＿＿＿＿＿＿＿＿2＿＿＿＿＿＿＿＿＿＿, in other words, to act. Well, this image, you've all seen. It changed our view of the physical world. We had never seen our planet from this perspective before. Many people credit a lot of the birth of the environmental movement to our seeing the planet like this for the first time, its smallness, its fragility 40 years later, this group, more than most, are well aware of the destructive power that our species can   wield over our environment. And at last, we appear to be doing something about it. ＿＿＿＿＿＿＿＿

＿＿＿＿＿＿＿＿＿3＿＿＿＿＿＿＿＿＿. For example, these images taken by Brent Stirton in the Congo, these gorillas were murdered, some would even say crucified, and unsurprisingly, they sparked international outrage. Most recently, we've been tragically reminded of the destructive power of nature itself with the recent earthquake in Haiti.

What I think that is far worse is man's destructive power over man. Samuel Pisar, an Auschwitz survivor said, and I'll quote him, "The Holocaust teaches us that nature, even in its cruelest moments, is benign in comparison with man, when he loses his moral compass and his reason."

There's another kind of crucifixion. The horrifying images from Abu Ghraib as well as the images from Guantanamo had a profound impact. The publication of those images, as opposed to the images themselves, caused a government to change its policies. Some would argue that it is those images that did more to fuel the insurgency in Iraq than virtually any other single act. Furthermore, those images forever removed the so-called moral high ground of the occupying forces.

Let's go back a little. In the 1960s and 1970s, the Vietnam War was basically shown in

America's living rooms day in, day out. News photos brought people face to face with the victims of the war, a little girl burned by napalm, a student killed by the National Guard at Kent State University in Ohio during a protest. In fact, these images became the voices of protest themselves. Now, _____ 4 _____, and in particular — I've given a lot of talks on this but I'll just show one image — the issue of HIV/AIDS. In the 1980s the stigmatization of people with the disease was an enormous barrier to even discussing or addressing it. A simple act, in 1987, of the most famous woman in the world, the Princess of Wales, touching an HIV/AIDS infected baby, did a great deal, especially in Europe, to stop that. She, better than most, knew the power of an image.

So when we are confronted by a powerful image, we all have a choice. We can look away, or we can address the image. Thankfully, when these photos appeared in the Guardian in 1998, they put a lot of focus and attention, and in the end a lot of money, towards the Sudan famine relief efforts. Did the images change the world? No, but they had a majo impact. _____5_____. We all saw those images after Katrina, and I think for millions of people, they had a very strong impact, and I think it's very unlikely that they were far from the minds of Americans when they went to vote in November 2008.

Unfortunately, some very important images are deemed too graphic or disturbing for us to see them. I'll show you one photo here, and it's a photo by Eugene Richards of an Iraq War veteran from an extraordinary piece of work, which has never been published, called "War is Personal." But images don't need to be graphic in order to remind us of the tragedy of war. John Moore set up this photo at Arlington cemetery. After all the tense moments of conflict, in all the conflict zones of the world, there's one photograph from a much quieter place that haunts me still, much more than the others.

Ansel Adams said, and I disagree with him, "You don't take a photograph, you make it." In my view, it's not the photographer who makes the photo, it's you. We bring to each image our own values, our own belief systems, and as a result of that, the image resonates with us. My company has 70 million images. I have one image in my office. Here it is. I hope that the next time you see an image that sparks something in you, you'll better understand why, and I know that, speaking to this audience, you'll definitely do something about it.

And thank you to all the photographers. (Applause)

1.4.2　Oral Practice—Debate

1. What is your understanding to this sentence "After all the tense moments of conflict, in all the conflict zones of the world, there's one photograph from a much quieter place that haunts me still, much more than the others" ?

2. What is the power of images ? What is the power of words?

3. Is the words more powerful than the images? In what way do you agree? Please illustrate your arguments.

1.5   Oral Enhancement Drills

1.5.1   Warming Up: Tongue Twisters

She sells seashells on the seashore.

The shells she sells are seashells, I'm sure.

For if she sells seashells on the seashore,

Then I'm sure she sells seashore shells.

1.5.2   Cultural Introduction

❖ **Background Information**

In the west, when two people first meet and are getting acquainted with each other, it is common to talk about one's work, aspects of one's social identity, including education, employment experience, technical and general knowledge, personal interests, family, routine activities, likes and dislikes, and leisure time activities.

Explain your name without using the words in your name and let your partner guess your name from your expression.

❖ **Ask the following questions:**

1. What's your given name?

2. Does your given name have a meaning in Chinese? What is it?

3. Is your name common in China?

4. Why did your parents choose this name for you?

5. Are you happy with your name? Why?

6. Did you like your name when you were a child?

7. Do you have a nickname? What is it?

8. What is your favorite name? Why?

❖ **Making up dialogues by using the information given below:**

1. A freshman meets a sophomore on campus; they greet each other and talk about their university life and studies.

2. Ask your partner to give you as much information as possible about his or her hometown, favorite city, field of study, family and friends, hobbies, favorite book and sports activities.

❖ **Discussions:**

1. What kind of people will you like and tend to accept at the first sight? List the qualities of welcome people in your mind. Check with yourself. Are you popular among your classmates?

2. Have you ever heard any interesting story about people's names?

1.5.3　Free Talk

1. How would you like your oral English class be delivered?
2. What are required to be good at oral English?

1.6　After-class Activities

1.6.1　Cultural Understanding

Video Appreciation : Disney

1. What's your favorite animation movie?
2. What do you think of cultural invasion?

1.6.2　Cultural Listening Comprehension

◇ **Section A**

Directions: In this section, you will hear two long conversations. At the end of each conversation, you will hear some questions. Both the conversation and the questions will be spoken only once. After you hear a question, you must choose the best answer from the four choices marked A), B), C) and D).

• **Conversation One**

Questions 1 to 4 are based on the conversation you have just heard.

1. A) A new art project in the city.
   B) An assignment for their art class.
   C) An art display inside the public library.
   D) A painting that the girl saw downtown.

2. A) A famous artist is going to visit his class.
   B) His artwork might be seen by many people.
   C) His class might visit an art museum.
   D) He is getting a good grade in his art class.

3. A) To the zoo.
   B) To an art store.
   C) To Main Street.
   D) To the public library.

4. A) So that he can hand in his homework.
   B) So that he can sign up for a class trip.
   C) So that he can see a new painting.

D) So that he can talk to the teacher.

- **Conversation Two**

Questions 5 to 8 are based on the conversation you have just heard.

5. A) She felt embarrassed in class.

    B) Her presentation received a poor grade.

    C) She had not completed her assignment.

    D) She was unable to attend her psychology class.

6. A) She'd be able to leave quickly.

    B) She'd be less nervous.

    C) She'd be able to locate where the man was seated.

    D) She'd know when her professor arrived.

7. A) They blush more readily than women do.

    B) They're uncomfortable performing in front of adults.

    C) They don't respond to stress well.

    D) They blush less frequently than adults do.

8. A) To introduce the woman to someone who has researched blushing.

    B) To illustrate the benefits of a public-speaking class.

    C) To give an example of someone who blushes easily.

    D) To explain a way to overcome blushing.

◇ Section B

Directions: In this section, you will hear two passages. At the end of each passage, you will hear some questions. Both the passage and the questions will be spoken only once. After you hear a question, you must choose the best answer from the four choices marked A), B), C) and D).

- **Passage One**

Questions 9 to 11 are based on the passage you have just heard.

9. A) It is affecting our health seriously.

    B) It hinders our reading and writing.

    C) It is changing our bodies as well as our culture.

    D) It surprises people with unexpected messages.

10. A) They must arrange the meeting place well in advance.

    B) They can postpone fixing the place till last minute.

    C) They needn't decide when and where to meet.

    D) They still have to work out detailed meeting plans.

11. A) The texts are the revealing of the texters' characters.

    B) The texts are well written by the texters.

    C) The texts are unacceptable by others expect the texters.

  D) The texts are shocking to others and the texter himself.

- **Passage Two**

Questions 12 to 15 are based on the passage you have just heard.

12. A) It has a personal style.

  B) It sounds very familiar to our ears.

  C) It is one whole style you cannot recognize.

  D) It does not belong to any composer.

13. A) It combines different feelings together.

  B) It can express some very confusing feelings.

  C) It exaggerates some special feelings.

  D) It expresses feelings in an appropriate way.

14. A) The newer the music is, the longer time it will last.

  B) It is easy for music to gain a permanent status.

  C) Good music always stands the test of time.

  D) Good music needn't be tested by time.

15. A) Pop music's biggest test is the test of time.

  B) Pop music's tunes do not have very clear styles.

  C) Pop music may not express any important feeling at all.

  D) Pop music may exaggerate some feelings.

◇ Section C

Directions: In this section, you will hear three recordings of lectures or talks followed by some questions. The recordings will be played only once. After you hear a question, you must choose the best answer from the four choices marked A), B), C) and D).

- **Recording One**

Questions 16 to 19 are based on the recording you have just heard.

16. A) It is when one has an attempt to buy with a good reason.

  B) It is when one recalls some past events and activities.

  C) It is when one enjoys seeing some images in his mind.

  D) It is when one gets a mental picture without consciousness.

17. A) Whether it proves worth the money spent.

  B) Whether it can create a mental impression.

  C) Whether it helps sell more of their products.

  D) Whether it can arouse anger in the audience.

18. A) It needs a cautious application.

  B) It has no effect on sales.

  C) It benefits the customers.

  D) It causes a mental confusion.

19. A) He reveals none in the passage.

　　B) He advocates its prohibition.

　　C) He considers it an exaggeration.

　　D) He acclaims its effectiveness.

- **Recording Two**

Questions 20 to 22 are based on the recording you have just heard.

20. A) No conservation of water.

　　B) Disease carried in water.

　　C) Poor economies.

　　D) Drinking unhealthy water.

21. A) To turn the faucet off when brushing your teeth.

　　B) To avoid give more flushes each time.

　　C) To replace the old toilet.

　　D) To make sure of the manufacturing date of the toilet.

22. A) Make the food colorful.

　　B) Check where the leaks are.

　　C) Plug the hole in the tank.

　　D) Decorate the bathroom.

- **Recording Three**

Questions 23 to 25 are based on the recording you have just heard.

23. A) The Yellow Room.

　　B) The Blue Room.

　　C) The Dining Room.

　　D) The Oval Office.

24. A) He built a bowling alley.

　　B) He formed a ping-pong team.

　　C) He built an indoor basketball court.

　　D) He built a movie theatre.

25. A) George Washington.

　　B) John Adams.

　　C) Richard Nixon.

　　D) Abraham Lincoln.

Chapter 2   Language and Culture

2.1   The Diversity of Culture

Cultural diversity is related to the cultural differences we have in a country, a society or to be at large in the world. We can see cultural diversity through the different languages people talk, the different body languages people have, the different religions or through the different types of foods for example. But cultural diversity is also simply people with a different age, sex, gender or different physical features.

It is great but above all necessary. It makes a country richer in creative minds and ideas. Cultural diversity leads to new thinking and solutions. People develop their human values and respect. Today, more and more companies try to hire people from different cultural backgrounds in order to create a cultural sensitivity and awareness. People from different cultural backgrounds also share different perspectives when it comes to brainstorming, which is for sure, valuable for all companies.

Many countries are largely populated by immigrants, and the culture is influenced by the many groups of people that now make up the country. This is also a part of growth. As the countries grow, so does its cultural diversity. A society with a huge variance of talent and perspectives will be more adaptive than one which is homogenous—where everyone is the same. This is because a changing environment in which the individuals can't change will always select out individuals who are less adaptive and will favor those who fit the needs of the times. So, the nation with the biggest population with the most variation will out compete those whose societal members are relatively similar. Cultural diversity makes a country richer by making it a more interesting place in which to live. Cultural diversity also makes one country stronger and better able to compete in the new global economy. People from diverse cultures bring language skills, new ways of thinking, creative solutions to difficult problems and negotiating skills. It is then obviously really valuable for people to travel, work abroad or merge themselves in new and different environments, in order to embrace that cultural diversity and to share new knowledge and ideas with others.

2.2   The Diversity of Language

How is Language Related to Culture

There are many ways in which the phenomena of language and culture are intimately related. Both phenomena are unique to humans and have therefore been the subject of a great deal of anthropological, sociological, and even mimetic study. Language, of course, is determined by culture, though the extent to which this is true is now under debate. The converse is also true to some degree: culture is determined by language—or rather, by the replicators that created both, memes.

Early anthropologists, following the theory that words determine thought, believed that language and its structure were entirely dependent on the cultural context in which they existed. This was a logical extension of what is termed the Standard Social Science Model, which views the human mind as an indefinitely malleable structure capable of absorbing any sort of culture without constraints from genetic or neurological factors.

In this vein, anthropologist Verne Ray conducted a study in the 1950's, giving color samples to different American Indian tribes and asking them to give the names of the colors. He concluded that the spectrum we see as "green", "yellow", etc. was an entirely arbitrary division, and each culture divided the spectrum separately. According to this hypothesis, the divisions seen between colors are a consequence of the language we learn, and do not correspond to divisions in the natural world. A similar hypothesis is upheld in the extremely popular meme of Eskimo words for snow—common stories vary from fifty to upwards of two hundred.

Extreme cultural relativism of this type has now been clearly refuted. Eskimos use at most twelve different words for snow, which is not many more than English speakers and should be expected since they exist in a cold climate. The color-relativity hypothesis has now been completely debunked by more careful, thorough, and systematic studies which show a remarkable similarity between the ways in which different cultures divide the spectrum.

Of course, there are ways in which culture really does determine language, or at least certain facets thereof. Obviously, the ancient Romans did not have words for radios, televisions, or computers because these items were simply not part of their cultural context. In the same vein, uncivilized tribes living in Europe in the time of the Romans did not have words for tribunes, praetors, or any other trapping of Roman government because Roman law was not part of their culture.

Our culture does, sometimes, restrict what we can think about efficiently in our own language. For example, some languages have only three color terms equivalent to black, white, and red; a native speaker of this language would have a difficult time expressing the concept of "purple" efficiently. Some languages are also more expressive about certain topics. For example, it is commonly acknowledged that Yiddish is a linguistic champion, with an amazing number of words referring to the simpleminded.

2.3　Pre-watching Activities

Video One: Hardest Languages

★　**New Words**

Mandarin 汉语	Hungarian 匈牙利语
Finnish 芬兰语	Estonian 爱沙尼亚语
Indo-European 印欧语系	Finno-Ugric 乌戈尔语系
line up 排列	prominently 突出地
Cantonese 广东话	archaic 古老的
ideograms 表意文字	graphic symbols 图形符号
literate 有读写能力的	Hangul 韩语字母
given 鉴于	simplified characters 简化字
Xhosa 科萨语	Bantu 班图语
Navajo 纳瓦霍语	code talker 密语者
missionary 传教士	reservation 保留地
momentaneous 瞬间	outwit 智胜
Eskimo　爱斯基摩	Inuit 因纽特人
conceptually　从概念上讲	

2.3.1　Compound Dictation One

How difficult a language is to learn is often_____1_____. For example, a Dutch speaker trying to learn German will have a much easier time than, say, a Mandarin speaker because Dutch and German are closely related languages and Mandarin and German are not, so get ready to find out about the 5 most difficult languages in the world to learn. Hungarian stands as several odd men out in Europe alongside Finnish and Estonian as belonging to a language family other than that of a majority of European languages. Most European languages belong to a family called Indo-European but Hungarian belongs to a family called Finno-Ugric. What makes Hungarian incredibly difficult to learn for say German or English speaker is _____2_____. For example, German and English have many words in common with each other, such as finger and Finger(德语), beer and bier(德语) and wolf and Wolf(德语). But if you line up those same words with Hungarian you can see where the difficulty comes in, finger and uii(匈牙利语), beer and sor(匈牙利语) and wolf and farkas(匈牙利语). They are completely different, making it a true challenge to learn. There really is no such thing as Chinese. Rather_____3_____ are in fact different languages. Mandarin is the official language of China, but there are others, most prominently the Cantonese language which is spoken in southern China as well as in Hong Kong and Macao. Mandarin has four different tones, each of which conveys a different meaning and can be difficult enough to get right for a foreigner but Cantonese has six tones. Additionally the real difficulty in learning Chinese is always the reading and writing system because the language has no alphabet._____4_____. Ideograms are graphic symbols that convey meaning and the Chinese ones were originally based on representation of things from the real world. Over time the relationship between the symbols and what they represented was lost, but the complexity in the number of characters grew._____5_____. Compare that to Korean alphabet Hangul which can be learned in a few hours and you get an idea of how difficult it can be to acquire even basic literacy. Given this the Chinese writing system was reformed in the twentieth century in mainland China into what is called simplified characters but in HK they kept the even more complex traditional ones which, when combined with a greater number of tones, _____6_____. Xhosa is a language that belongs to the African family of languages called Bantu and it is one of the official languages of South Africa. In addition to a difficult grammar and vocabulary foreign to native speakers of English, it is one of _____7_____ in order to pronounce correctly. The language has totaled 18 clicks that are very hard for non-natives to learn. So if you decide to pick up Xhosa, all we can say is Good Luck. You are going to need it. Navajo is an American Indian language and it has an unusual role in history due to its isolation as a language and small number of speakers. During WWII a man named Philip Johnston suggested the introduction of so-called Navajo code talkers in order to _____8_____. He was fortunate to grow up as a son of missionary in a reservation and thus spoke it fluently. But he also realized that almost no one spoke it and those who tried usually failed. Considering its distinguishing tense which refers to when something happened as we do in English, Navajo instead uses something called ASPECT which _____9_____. These have no real correspondence in English but of classifications such as transitional which involves action involving transition from one status of a form to another momentaneous which involves the action that takes place at a specific point of time and many others. You can see why Nava beheld and learned and why the Novojo code talkers were able to _____10_____. If you thought Navajo will be hard to learn, then Greenlandic is just off the charts. It's one of the Eskimo languages spoken by the Inuit of Greenland and its incredibly strange and difficult grammar makes it the most difficult language to learn. Besides being unrelated to anything western or eastern people are familiar with, it is the grammar that is the real killer. Most languages have distinctive parts for subjects, objects and verbs, but in Greenlandic _____11_____ including the subject and object, making the language conceptually very different from anything you might have encountered in a language learning classroom.

2.3.2   Conversation Practice

1. Do you think English is difficult to learn? Why or why not?
2. Do you know any other language that is incredibly difficult to learn?

2.4　Watching Activities

Video Two: Don't Insist on English

★　New Words

unprecedented 前所未有的	undisputed 不可置疑的
empower 授权，使能够	morph 变体
bandwagon 时尚	segment 狭隘的部分
arbitrary 武断的	remedial 需要补习的
prohibitive 禁止的	kerosene lamp 煤油灯

2.4.1　Compound Dictation Two

I know what you're thinking. You think I've lost my way. Somebody's going to come on the stage in a minute and guide me gently back to my seat. (Applause) I get that all the time in Dubai. "Here on the holiday are you, dear?" (Laughter) "Come to visit the children? How long are you staying?" Well actually, I hope for a while longer yet. I have been living and teaching in the Gulf for over 30 years. (Applause) And in that time, I have seen a lot of changes. Now that statistic is quite shocking. And I want to talk to you today _____1_____. I want to tell you about my friend who was teaching English to adults in Abu Dhabi. And one fine day, she decided to take them into the garden to teach them some nature vocabulary. But it was she who ended up learning all the Arabic words for the local plants, as well as their uses, medicinal uses, cosmetics(化妆用的), cooking, herbal(草本的). How did those students get all that knowledge? Of course, from their grandparents and even their great-grandparents. It's not necessary to tell you _____2_____. But sadly, today,_____3_____. A language dies every 14 days. Now, at the same time, _____4_____. Could there be a connection? Well I don't know. But I do know that I've seen a lot of changes. When I first came out to the Gulf, I came to Kuwait in the days when it was still a hardship post. Actually, not that long ago. That is a little bit too early. But nevertheless, I was recruited by the British Council, along with about 25 other teachers. And we were the first non-Muslims to teach in the state schools there in Kuwait. We were brought to teach English because the government wanted to modernize the country and to empower(授权，使能够) the citizens through education. And of course, the U.K. benefited from some of that lovely oil wealth.

Okay. Now this is the major change that I've seen-how teaching English has morphe(变体)

5

that it is today. No longer just a foreign language on the school curriculum(课程), and no longer the sole domain(唯一的领域) of mother England, it has become a bandwagon for every

English-speaking nation on earth. And why not? After all, the best education—according to the latest World University Rankings(等级，排名)—is to be found in the universities of the U.K. and the U.S. So everybody wants to have an English education naturally. But if you're not a native speaker, you have to pass a test. Now _____6_____? Perhaps you have a computer scientist who's a genius. Would he need the same language as a lawyer, for example? Well, I don't think so. We English teachers reject them all the time. We put a stop sign and we stop them in their tracks. They can't pursue their dream any longer till they get English. Now let me put it this way: if I met a monolingual Dutch speaker who had the cure for cancer, would I stop him from entering my British University? I don't think so. But indeed, that is exactly what we do. We English teachers are the gatekeepers(看门人). And you have to satisfy us first that your English is good enough. _____7_____.

Okay. "But," I hear you say, "what about the research? It's all in English." So the books are in English, the journals are done in English, but that is a self-fulfilling(自我实现的) prophecy(预言能力). It feeds the English requirement. And so it goes on. I ask you, what happened to translation? _____8_____. They translated from Latin and Greek into Arabic, into Persian, and then it was translated on into the Germanic languages of Europe and the Romance languages. And so _____9_____.

Now don't get me wrong; I am not against teaching English, all you English teachers out there. I love it that we have a global language. We need one today more than ever But _____10_____. Do we really want to end up with 600 languages and the main one being English , or Chinese? We need more than that. Where do we draw the line? This system _____11_____. (Applause) And I want to remind you that the giants upon whose shoulders today's intelligentsia stand did not have to pass an English test. Case in point, Einstein. He, by the way, was considered remedial at school because he was, in fact, dyslexic(读写困难). But fortunately for the world, he did not have to pass an English test. Because they didn't start until 1964 with TOEFL, the American test of English. Now it's exploded. There are lots and lots of tests of English. And millions and millions of students take these tests every year. Now you might think, you and me, "Those fees aren't bad, they're okay," but _____12_____(禁止的) to so many millions of poor people. So immediately, we're rejecting them. (Applause)

It brings to mind a headline I saw recently: "_____13_____" Now I get it, I understand why people would want to focus on English. They want to give their children the best chance in life. And to do that, they need a Western education. Because, of course, the best jobs go to people out of the Western Universities, that I put on earlier. It's a circular thing.

Okay. Let me tell you a story about two scientists, two English scientists. They were doing an experiment to do with genetics and the forelimbs and the hind limbs(前肢和后肢) of animals. But they couldn't get the results they wanted. They really didn't know what to do, until along came a German scientist who realized that they were using two words for forelimb and hind limb, whereas genetics does not differentiate and neither does German. So bingo ,problem solved. _____14_____.

My daughter came to England from Kuwait. She had studied science and mathematics in Arabic. It's an Arabic medium school. She had to translate it into English at her grammar school. And she was the best in the class at those subjects. Which tells us that when students come to us from abroad, we may not be giving them enough credit (荣誉，信任)for what they know, and they know it in their own language. _____15_____.

This is — I don't know if you saw it on CNN recently — they gave the Heroes Award to a young Kenyan shepherd(牧羊的) boy who couldn't study at night in his village, like all the village children, because the kerosene lamp(煤油灯). It had smoke and it damaged his eyes. And anyway, there was never enough kerosene, because what does a dollar a day buy for you? So he invented a cost-free solar lamp. And now _____16_____. And when…(Applause) When he received his award, he said these lovely words: "The children can lead Africa from what it is today, a dark continent, to a light continent." A simple idea, but it could have such far-reaching consequences. People who have no light, whether it's physical or metaphorical （隐喻性的), cannot pass our exams, and we can never know what they know. Let us not keep them and ourselves in the dark. _____17_____. (Applause)

Thank you very much.

2.4.2　Oral Practice—Debate

1. What are the advantages and disadvantages of English becoming a global language?
2. What can be done to protect language diversity in the era of globalization?
3. Is it possible for Mandarin to be adopted as a global language? Please illustrate your arguments.

2.5　Oral Enhancement Drills

2.5.1　Warming Up: Tongue Twisters

Peter Piper picked a peck of pickled peppers.
A peck of pickled peppers Peter Piper picked.
If Peter Piper picked a peck of pickled peppers,
Where's the peck of pickled peppers Peter Piper picked?

2.5.2　Cultural Introduction

❖ **Background Information**

In the west, people will go Dutch while having a meal in the restaurant. They usually don't entertain guests. Even when they are invited to a friend's birthday party, they would not expect a free main dish from the birthday person.

❖ **Ask the following questions:**

1. Do you split the bill when you go out to eat with your friends?

2. Who do you think should settle the bill on the first date, girl or guy?

3. Does the woman have to pay during the dating period, like 4 or 5 months of dating?

4. What would you think if your boyfriend pays for you every time?

5. What would you think if your girlfriend never offers to pay when you go out? Would you feel like you are taken advantage of?

❖ **Making up dialogues by using the information given below:**

1. You want to take a girl out for dinner for the first time but you don't have enough money, so you ask your sister for help, who suggests letting the girl pay.

2. After the meal, both of you expect the other to pay and give a lot of reasons to explain why.

❖ **Discussions:**

1. Do you agree that it is a gesture of respect to let the girl pay for her share on the first date in this era of gender equality?

2. What are your parents' opinions of going Dutch?

2.5.3 Free Talk

1. Do you think money can buy love?

2. What do you think of a couple who go Dutch for everything?

2.6 After-class Activities

2.6.1 Cultural Understanding

Video Appreciation : My Big Fat Greek Wedding

1. What cause the difficulties in Tuola and Ian's relationship and marriage?

2. What do you think of cross-culture marriage? What would make a successful intercultural marriage?

2.6.2 Cultural Listening Comprehension

◇ **Section A**

Directions: In this section, you will hear two long conversations. At the end of each conversation, you will hear four questions. Both the conversation and the questions will be spoken only once. After you hear a question, you must choose the best answer. from the four choices marked A), B),C) and D).

· Conversation One

Questions 1 to 4 are based on the conversation you have just heard.

1. A) The project the man managed at CucinTech.
   B) The updating of technology at CucinTech.
   C) The man's switch to a new career.
   D) The restructuring of her company.

2. A) Talented personnel.
   B) Strategic innovation.
   C) Competitive products.
   D) Effective promotion.

3. A) Expand the market.
   B) Recruit more talents.
   C) Innovate constantly.
   D) Watch out for his competitors.

4. A) Possible bankruptcy.
   B) Unforeseen difficulties.
   C) Conflicts within the company.
   D) Imitation by one's competitors.

· Conversation Two

Questions 5 to 8 are based on the conversation you have just heard.

5. A) The job of an interpreter.
   B) The stress felt by professionals.
   C) The importance of language proficiency.
   D) The best way to effective communication.

6. A) Promising.
   B) Admirable.
   C) Rewarding.
   D) Meaningful.

7. A) They all have a strong interest in language.
   B) They all have professional qualifications.
   C) They have all passed language proficiency tests.
   D) They have all studied cross-cultural differences.

8. A) It requires a much larger vocabulary.
   B) It attaches more importance to accuracy.
   C) It is more stressful than simultaneous interpreting.

D) It puts one's long-term memory under more stress.

◇ Section B

Directions: In this section, you will hear two passages. At the end of each passage, you will hear three or four questions. Both the passage and the questions will be spoken only once. After you hear a question, you must choose the best answer from the four choices marked A), B), C) and D).

· **Passage One**

Questions 9 to 12 are based on the passage you have just heard.

9. A) It might affect mothers' health.

    B) It might disturb infants' sleep.

    C) It might increase the risk of infants, death.

    D) It might increase mothers' mental distress.

10. A) Mothers who breast-feed their babies have a harder time falling asleep.

    B) Mothers who sleep with their babies need a little more sleep each night.

    C) Sleeping patterns of mothers greatly affect their newborn babies' health.

    D) Sleeping with infants in the same room has a negative impact on mothers.

11. A) Change their sleep patterns to adapt to their newborn babies'.

    B) Sleep in the same room but not in the same bed as their babies.

    C) Sleep in the same house but not in the same room as their babies.

    D) Take precautions to reduce the risk of sudden infant death syndrome.

· **Passage Two**

Questions 12 to 15 are based on the passage you have just heard.

12. A) A lot of native languages have already died out in the US.

    B) The US ranks first in the number of endangered languages.

    C) The efforts to preserve Indian languages have proved fruitless.

    D) More money is needed to record the native languages in the US.

13. A) To set up more language schools.

    B) To document endangered languages.

    C) To educate native American children.

    D) To revitalise America's native languages.

14. A) The US govemment's policy of Americanising Indian children.

    B) The failure of American Indian languages to gain an official status.

    C) The US government's unwillingness to spend money educating Indians.

    D) The long-time isolation of American Indians from the outside world.

15. A) It is being utilised to teach native languages.

    B) It tells traditional stories during family time.

    C) It speeds up the extinction of native languages.

D) It is widely used in language immersion schools.

◇ Section C

Directions: In this section, you will hear three recordings of lectures or talks followed by three or four questions. The recordings will be played only once. After you hear a question, you must choose the best answer from the four choices marked A), B), C) and D).

· **Recording One**

Questions 16 to 19 are based on the recording you have just heard.

16. A) It pays them up to half of their previous wages while they look for work.

　　B) It covers their mortgage payments and medical expenses for 99 weeks.

　　C) It pays their living expenses until they find employment again.

　　D) It provides them with the basic necessities of everyday life.

17. A) Creating jobs for the huge army of unemployed workers.

　　B) Providing training and guidance for unemployed workers.

　　C) Convincing local lawmakers to extend unemployment benefits.

　　D) Raising funds to help those having no unemployment insurance.

18. A) To offer them loans they need to start their own businesses.

　　B) To allow them to postpone their monthly mortgage payments.

　　C) To create more jobs by encouraging private investments in local companies.

　　D) To encourage big businesses to hire back workers with government subsidies.

· **Recording Two**

Questions 19 to 22 are based on the recording you have just heard.

19. A) They measured the depths of sea water.

　　B) They analyzed the water content.

　　C) They explored the ocean floor.

　　D) They investigated the ice.

20. A) Eighty percent of the ice disappears in summer time.

　　B) Most of the ice was accumulated over the past centuries.

　　C) The ice ensures the survival of many endangered species.

　　D) The ice decrease is more evident than previously thought.

21. A) Arctic ice is a major source of the world's fresh water.

　　B) The melting Arctic ice has drowned many coastal cities.

　　C) The decline of Arctic ice is irreversible.

　　D) Arctic ice is essential to human survival.

22. A) It will do a lot of harm to mankind.

　　B) There is no easy way to understand it.

　　C) It will advance nuclear technology.

　　D) There is no easy technological solution to it.

- **Recording Three**

Questions 23 to 25 are based on the recording you have just heard.

23. A) The reason why New Zealand children seem to have better self-control.

    B) The relation between children's self-control and their future success.

    C) The health problems of children raised by a single parent.

    D) The deciding factor in children's academic performance.

24. A) Children raised by single parents will have a hard time in their thirties.

    B) Those with a criminal record mostly come from single parent families.

    C) Parents must learn to exercise self-control in front of their children.

    D) Lack of self-control in parents is a disadvantage for their children.

25. A) Self-control can be improved through education.

    B) Self-control can improve one's financial situation.

    C) Self-control problems may be detected early in children.

    D) Self-control problems will diminish as one grows up.

Chapter 3　Cultural Value Orientations

3.1　Culture Shock and Adaptation

Culture shock is an experience a person may have when one moves to a cultural environment which is different from one's own; it is also the personal disorientation a person may feel when experiencing an unfamiliar way of life due to immigration or a visit to a new country, a move between social environments, or simply transition to another type of life. One of the most common causes of culture shock involves individuals in a foreign environment. Culture shock can be described as consisting of at least one of four distinct phases: honeymoon, negotiation, adjustment, and adaptation.

Common problems include: information overload, language barrier, generation gap, technology gap, skill interdependence, formulation dependency, homesickness (cultural), infinite regress (homesickness), boredom (job dependency), response ability (cultural skill set). There is no true way to entirely prevent culture shock, as individuals in any society are personally affected by cultural contrasts differently.

Academically, culture adaptation is one of the content of cultural relativism in anthropology, which is used for culture studies. Culture adaptation refers to the process of acclimatizing to the demand of new cultural environment. The adaptation process includes the excitement about the new situation, confusion when faced with the hidden aspect of culture, frustration when old ways of dealing with situations that fails to work, growing effectiveness as new skills are acquired, appreciation as new skills and attitudes enable to live more fully in the new situation and increased ability to deal with new and novel situation.

3.2　Norms of Social Interaction

Social norms, the customary rules that govern behavior in groups and societies, have been extensively studied in the social sciences. Anthropologists have described how social norms function in different cultures (Geertz 1973), sociologists have focused on their social functions and how they motivate people to act (Durkheim 1950; Parsons 1937, Parsons and Shils 1951; Coleman 1990; Hechter and Opp 2001), and economists have explored how adherence to norms influences market behavior (Akerlof 1976; Young 1998). More recently, also legal scholars have touted social norms as efficient alternatives to legal rules, as they may internalize negative externalities and provide signaling mechanisms at little or no cost (Ellickson 1991; Posner 2000).

With a few exceptions, the social science literature conceives of norms as exogenous variables. Since norms are mainly seen as constraining behavior, some of the important differences between moral, social and legal norms, as well as differences between norms and conventions, have been blurred. Much attention instead has been paid to the conditions under which norms will be obeyed. Because of that, the issue of sanctions has been paramount in the social science literature. Moreover, since social norms are seen as central to the production of social order or social coordination, research on norms has been focused on the functions they perform, and whether they do so efficiently. Yet even if a norm may fulfill important social functions such as welfare maximization or the elimination of externalities, it cannot be explained solely or mainly on the basis of the functions it performs. The simplistic functionalist perspective has been rejected on several accounts since, even if a given norm can be conceived as a means to achieve some social goal, this is usually not the reason why it emerged in the first place (Elster 1989). Moreover, though a particular norm may persist (as opposed to emerge) because of some positive social function it fulfills, there are many others that are inefficient and even widely unpopular.

Philosophers have taken a different approach to norms. In the literature on norms and conventions, both social constructs are seen as the endogenous product of individuals' interactions (Lewis 1969; Ullmann-Margalit 1977; Vandershraaf 1995; Bicchieri 2006). Norms are represented as equilibria of games of strategy, and as such they are supported by a cluster of self-fulfilling expectations. Beliefs, expectations, group knowledge and common knowledge have thus become central concepts in the development of a philosophical view of social norms. Paying attention to the role played by expectations in supporting social norms has helped differentiate between social norms, conventions, and descriptive norms, an important distinction often overlooked in the social science accounts.

3.3   Pre-watching Activities

Video One: Russia vs American German vs Greek

★ **New Words**

affront 冒犯	encroachment 侵犯
proxy 代理人	ineffectual 无效的, 不起作用的
annexation 合并	Crimea 克里米亚
subjugate 征服	conspiratorial 阴谋的
South Ossetia 南奥塞梯	genocide 种族灭绝
Euromaidan 欧洲广场	orchestrate 精心安排

Ivying 竞争的	vilify 诽谤
pew 座位，公众	austerity 紧缩；朴素
bail out 保释，跳伞	Ottoman 土耳其帝国的
eposition 处置	bode 预示
retaliation 报复	war reparation 战争赔款

3.3.1　Compound Dictation One

In August 2015,_____1_____. These actions have served as an affront to western countries like the United States which has spent much of the last century locked in battles with the Soviets. A 2015 poll found that more than 80% of Russians have negative opinions about the United States compared to 34% in 2012. So why does Russia hate the United States? Well, since the Russian Revolution in 1917 when the U.S. supported the anti communist side, Russia and the US have been _____2_____. Numerous territorial encroachment, proxy wars, and alternating alliances have set the stages for both countries to fear each other's imperialist goals. In recent years, Russian President Vladimir Putin has called the United States a parasite, living off the global economy. Throughout Russia, Americans are given the nickname "pindos" that suggested that _____3_____. This break in relations can in part be attributed to the US's push for sanctions following Russia's annexation of Crimea. A number of problems with Russia's economy, including the collapse of their currency and their inability to borrow money are the result of US involvement. Amongst Russian citizens, prices for food and basic goods have dramatically increased. Last year, Russia's economy grew barely half a percent, compared to 4.5% in 2010. Russia is also majorly unhappy ____4____. They see the increased in military bases and personnel as a method of keeping Russia subjugated. There is a considerate amount of propaganda coming from both Russia stated controlled media sources and long held conspiratorial beliefs about the United States. Many Russians believe that the events of 9/11 was planned by US government in order to invade the Middle East. And roughly 40% of the Russians don't believe that the US ever even landed on the moon. Analysts have also said that Russian hatred of the US is calculated to strengthen Russian foreign policy. In situations like the 2008 South Ossetia war, Russian accused US of supporting the genocide of Ossetians. However, numerous reports claimed that Russia started the conflict themselves. Russia also said that the 2013 Euromaidan protests in the Kiev before the annexation of Crimea were orchestrated by American forces and not simple local civil unrest. _____

_____5_____,the US and Russia are both vying for greater influence. This divide has made Russia an even more vilified figure around the world than the US. A recent pew poll has found that nearly every country has a very low confidence in Vladimir Putin with most negative ratings passing 75%. Even in the Middle East, President Brack Obama polled with a higher favorability than Putin. So why does Russia hate the US? _____6_____ have all made for an extremely hostile situation.

In July 2015, Greece voted against further austerity measures _____7_____. This move has continued to strain the relationship between Greece and Germany as a two major players in the EU's debt crisis. But this isn't the first time _____8_____. So why do Greece and Germany hate each other? The two country's difficult relationship can actually be traced back to modern Greece's beginnings. In the 1830s, Greece finally established itself as independent from the Ottoman Empire. The first ruler was Otto from Bavaria, a German State. However Otto was still a teenager at the time, so Greece was actually ruled by three other Bavarians, who were not welcomed by the Greeks. This eventually led to King Otto's __9__ and the Queen's _____10_____. This rocky start didn't bode well for the future of their relationship. Fast forward to World War II, _____11_____, the following German occupation led to _____12_____. Over million Greeks were made homeless and Greece's banks were drained to fund the war. In 1944, _____13_____ the deaths of seven Nazi soldiers. Greece's grievances concerning this event have continued till today. In 1960, Germany _____14_____ and said they owned them no more. _____15_____ and the debate continued for decades. In 1997, a Greek court found that Germany was responsible for further compensation for 1944 massacre. However, in 2012, the Hague ruled that German was immune from foreign lawsuits, sparking the ire of Greek citizens. Today the two countries continue to be at odds over the money Greece owes its creditors. The Greek Prime Minister argued that the amount of money due to them reparations would cover a significant portion of the debt in question. Greece has threatened to seize German property to pay for the alleged reparations. Meanwhile, Germany and the rest of the euro zone are desperate to find a solution that keeps the EU economy from collapsing from Greece's inflexibility. _____16_____.

3.3.2   Conversation Practice

1. Why do the US and Russia dislike each other according to the video clip?

2. What does the conflict between Greece and German result from?

3. Can you give other examples of countries that are on unfriendly terms because of history?

3.4   Watching Activities

Video Two: The Gua Sha Treatment

★ **New Words**

coloration 着色；染色	afflict 折磨；使痛苦
chitchat 聊天；闲谈	the defense 被告方

cutting-edge 尖端；前沿	craft 工艺；手艺
ooze 渗出；泄漏	steep 不合理的；夸大的
compassionate 富于同情心的	furnace 熔炉
obstreperous 难驾驭的	thermal dynamical principle 热动力学原理
capillary 毛细管	

3.4.1　Compound Dictation Two

Q (Mr. Quinlin): These accusations are incredibly ridiculous and laughable.

W (woman from the Child Welfare Agency): Perhaps you don't understand your friend. According to the doctor's report,_____1_____ when afflicted two days prior to Danis' head injury, we believe these photographs have sufficient evidence to demonstrate Danis Xu lives in dangerous home environment and should remain under the protection of the State.

J (judge): Please return to your seats.

Q: How could you do this to your son? Is this something you forgot to make me know? You know that no one will notice your son's back. _____2_____.

X (Xu Datong): That is Gua sha, _____3_____. Danis had a stomachache that day and Gua sha is simple a cure, a home remedy you call it. _____4_____.

Q: If you call it some kind of treatment, what do you see to consider child abuse?

J: If you two want to chitchat, we can all go home. Does the defense have something more to add?

W: No.

X: Yes, I do. I think you don't understand .You know Gua sha is a traditional Chinese medical treatment used for nearly all kinds of illness. For thousands of years, Chinese medicine recognized that there are seven "Jing" and eight "Mai". An example, _____5_____. A person's body has an invisible but very complex system of vessel network just like the computer network and also, the human "Qi" from Tan tien finally goes through Tan tien. It's the same principle.

J: He's your client. What did he say? _____6_____. Perhaps try another way, Mr. Xu. What does it say on every Missouri license plate?

X: "Show Me State".

J: Precisely! Can you get _____7_____ that a country judge can understand?

X: Yes, I can try.

P (Prosecutor): All right, Mr Quinlin. Let's get straight to the point, shall we? Mr Xu is an employee of Meantime New Media and also your best friend, right?

Q (Mr. Quinlin): Yes, he is an employee and I am proud to call Mr Xu my friend.

P: In what sort of business is Meantime New Media engaged?

Q: We design and distribute video games.

P: Quite true. You are known in your industry for the cutting-edge technology and high quality crafts. And I happen to have some of your games...

Q: What a coincidence.

P: "Death Quest", "Hell Races", "Malcolm's Massacre"

Q: We also created "Dream Seekers", "The Sally Says Educational Series".

P: But you were taken by concerned citizens' protest against excessively violent contents in your goals, were you?

Q: Those groups target all the video game designers.

P: That maybe. But Meantime New Media consistently in industry leagued in violence complaints, I also have a few video captured scenes from some of your most popular games. The graphics are astonishingly realistic. Like this "Guardian of the Universe" character, who punches his fist straight through his enemy's chest. And this one, when the hero delivers a single kick, his enemy's head splits open, brains oozing out.

J: Is this charming little show going anywhere?

P: Who created and designed these images?

Q: _____8_____.

P: Yes, but someone has to initiate the creative vision for the game. Yes, someone recently received an award for his video game design, especially for his design of ____9____. And that someone would be...

Q: Datong Xu.

P: If you may take one look at the work Datong Xu is engaged in day in and day out, you see this is _____10_____.

X. Culture of violence? The character in my latest video is adapted from ancient Chinese storyteller. _____11_____.

P: Oh, traditional values and ethics, Mr. Xu?

W: Burton, you don't have to play our part.

P: We do, if we want to hit a home run, sweetheart.

P: Now I read *Journey to the West* in English, the book this character is drawn from. Here is the story where peaches that take nine thousand years to harvest are our entrusted to Sun Wukong. Yet this typical Chinese monkey appropriated the entire harvest for himself. And when the poor farmers resist him, he totally destroyed their orchard...Here is another example of this creature's value system. _____
_____12_____.

X: That's nonsense!

P: Now it's such an obstreperous rude Chinese monkey. It's what Mr. Xu refers to as examples of values and morals.

X: What do you think what you are? You know nothing about Chinese culture!

D (Doctor): Gua sha, has a history of more than two thousand years in China. In most cases, illness that acupuncture and message are able to treat can be helped with Gua sha as well. Gua sha work according to the thermal dynamical principle that heat opens, cold closes. Does it hurt?

Q (Mr. Quinlin): Well, not.

D: With Gua sha, you can open up the blood capillary. How does it feel now?

Q: A little bit hot.

D: Hence, _____13_____, and has a health, restoring effect of reestablishing body's nature by biological circulation. All right, all done. Why don't you have a look in the mirror? _____14_____?

Q: I understand now. Thank you so much, doctor.

3.4.2　Oral Practice—Debate

1. What are the cultural shocks presented in the video clip? What causes these different understandings?

2. Does one's exposure to foreign culture strengthen one's cultural identity or undermines it please illustrate your point with evidence.

3.5　Oral Enhancement Drills

3.5.1　Warming Up: English Riddles

❖ **Read the following English language riddles and test out your reading comprehension and reasoning by trying to work out the answer:**

1. Who succeeded the first Prime Minister of Australia ? (key: second)

2. Why is the letter E like London? (key: Because E is the capital of England)

3. What part of the body has the most rhythm? (key: eardrums)

4. At night they come without being fetched, and by day they are lost without being stolen.(key: stars)

3.5.2　Cultural Introduction

❖ **Background Information**

In the west, arriving on time for appointments and events is important. If you agree to meet someone at a social event at 6:00 pm and you arrive later than 6:15 pm, many Americans consider this rude or impolite. People are expected to be on time for appointments, classes, and formal social events.

If you will be late, you should call the hosts and let them know that you will be delayed.

This preoccupation with time may also cause Americans to appear to be impatient and abrupt when they encounter delays.

❖ **Ask the following questions:**

1. Describe a situation when you are late.
2. When did this happen?
3. What occasion were you late for?
4. How did you explain your lateness?
5. Explain the result of your being late.
6. How do you feel about those guys who are always late?
7. What are normally the main reasons for being late?

❖ **Making up dialogues by using the information given below:**

1. Suppose you are a student late for your English class. Your teacher is a bit upset about it and you have to explain why you can't be in class on time.
2. You and your friend have an appointment.

❖ **Discussions:**

1. Have you heard any stories about people who have a narrow escape from a tragic event because of being late?
2. What are the ridiculous reasons people can give when they explain why they are late?

3.5.3   Free Talk

1. Where would you choose to go if you can afford going wherever you want to?
2. What do you think of shoestring travel?

3.6   After-class Activities

3.6.1   Cultural Understanding

Video Appreciation: Understanding the Rise of China

1. How is China going to change the world?
2. How is China different from western countries?
3. How does the west world misunderstand the rise of China?

3.6.2   Cultural Listening Comprehension

◇ **Section A**

Directions: In this section, you will hear two long conversations. At the end of each conversation, you will hear four questions. Both the conversation and the questions will be spoken only once. After you hear a question, you must choose the best answer. from the four choices marked A), B),C) and D).

- **Conversation One**

Questions 1 to 4 are based on the conversation you have just heard.

1. A) It is advertising electronic products.
   B) It is planning to tour East Asia.
   C) It is sponsoring a TV programme.
   D) It is giving performances in town.

2. A) 20,000 pounds.
   B) 12,000 pounds.
   C) Less than 20,000 pounds.
   D) Less than 12,000 pounds.

3. A) A lot of good publicity.
   B) Talented artists to work for it.
   C) Long-term investments.
   D) A decrease in production costs.

4. A) Promise long-term cooperation with the Company.
   B) Explain frankly their own current financial situation.
   C) Pay for the printing of the performance programme.
   D) Bear the cost of publicising the Company's performance.

- **Conversation Two**

Questions 5 to 8 are based on the conversation you have just heard.

5. A) He has been seeing doctors and counsellors.
   B) He has found a new way to train his voice.
   C) He was caught abusing drugs.
   D) He might give up concert tours.

6. A) Singers may become addicted to it.
   B) It helps singers warm themselves up.
   C) Singers use it to stay away from colds.
   D) It can do harm to singers' vocal chords.

7. A) They are eager to become famous.
   B) Many lack professional training.
   C) Few will become successful.
   D) They live a glamorous life.

8. A) Harm to singers done by smoky atmospheres.
   B) Side effects of some common drugs.
   C) Voice problems among pop singers.

D) Hardships experienced by many young singers.

◇ Section B

Directions: In this section, you will hear two passages. At the end of each passage, you will hear three or four questions. Both the passage and the questions will be spoken only once. After you hear a question, you must choose the best answer from the four choices marked A), B), C) and D).

- **Passage One**

Questions 9 to 12 are based on the passage you have just heard.

9. A) It has not been very successful
   B) It has long become a new trend.
   C) It has met with strong resistance.
   D) It has attracted a lot of users.

10. A) It saves time.
    B) It increases parking capacity.
    C) It ensures drivers' safety.
    D) It reduces car damage.

11. A) Collect money and help new users.
    B) Maintain the automated system.
    C) Stay alert to any emergency.
    D) Walk around and guard against car theft.

12. A) They will vary with the size of vehicles.
    B) They will be discountable to regular customers.
    C) They will be lower than conventional parking.
    D) They will be reduced if paid in cash.

- **Passage Two**

Questions 13 to 15 are based on the passage you have just heard.

13. A) They do not know any solution.
    B) They do not give up drunk driving.
    C) They do not behave in public places.
    D) They do not admit being alcohol addicts.

14. A) To stop them from fighting back.
    B) To thank them for their hospitality.
    C) To teach them the European lifestyle.
    D) To relieve their pains and sufferings.

15. A) Without intervention they will be a headache to the nation.
    B) With support they can be brought back to a normal life.
    C) They readily respond to medical treatment.

D) They pose a serious threat to social stability.

◇ Section C

Directions: In this section, you will hear three recordings of lectures or talks followed by three or four questions. The recordings will be played only once. After you hear a question, you must choose the best answer from the four choices marked A),B),C) and D).

- **Recording One**

Questions 16 to 19 are based on the recording you have just heard.

16. A) To award them for their hard work.
    B) To build common views.
    C) To bring in business projects.
    D) To vote for action.

17. A) Recovering from the Great Recession.
    B) Creating jobs and boosting the economy.
    C) Rewarding innovative businesses.
    D) Launching economic campaigns.

18. A) Talking over paying off deficit.
    B) Increasing the number of middle class.
    C) Controlling the impact on education.
    D) Planning to reduce energy consumption.

19. A) Shorten America's way to prosperity.
    B) Be cautious about reducing the deficit.
    C) Increase deficit to cover the revenue.
    D) Require the richest to pay more taxes.

- **Recording Two**

Questions 20 to 22 are based on the recording you have just heard.

20. A) They can be redeemed for cash.
    B) They can be used to reduce meal costs.
    C) They can be used as membership certificate.
    D) They can be used to make reservations.

21. A) It is free for us to download the app.
    B) It helps you to be a professional cook.
    C) It provides advice about making recipes.
    D) It only rates recipes by popularity.

22. A) By showing the weight of 200 kinds of food.
    B) By providing the price of 200 calories of food.
    C) By picturing the food of 200 calories with weights.
    D) By telling people 200 kinds of healthy food.

- **Recording Three**

Questions 23 to 25 are based on the recording you have just heard.

23. A) About 43 percent of American adults.

    B) About 18 percent of the whole population.

    C) About 40 million American adults.

    D) About a half million people in America.

24. A) To set a series of bans on public smoking.

    B) To set the price of cigarettes properly.

    C) To package the cigarettes with tips of warning.

    D) To reduce the production and supply of cigarettes.

25. A) The office of the Surgeon General.

    B) The Food and Drug Administration.

    C) The Center for Tobacco Products.

    D) The Center for Disease Control and Prevention.

Chapter 4　Intercultural Insight

4.1　Cultural Dimensions

Hofsted's cultural dimensions theory is a framework for cross-cultural communication, developed by Geert Hofstede. It describes the effects of a society's culture on the values of its members, and how these values relate to behavior, using a structure derived from factor analysis.

Hofstede developed his original model as a result of using factor analysis to examine the results of a world-wide survey of employee values by IBM between 1967 and 1973. It has been refined since. The original theory proposed four dimensions along which cultural values could be analyzed: individualism—collectivism; uncertainty avoidance; power distance (strength of social hierarchy) and masculinity—femininity (task orientation versus person-orientation). Independent research in Hong Kong led Hofstede to add a fifth dimension, long-term orientation, to cover aspects of values not discussed in the original paradigm. In 2010, Hofstede added a sixth dimension, indulgence versus self-restraint.

4.1.1　Individualism—Collectivism

This dimension focuses on the relationship between the individual and larger social groups. As mentioned earlier, cultures vary on the amount of emphasis they give on encouraging individuality uniqueness or on conformity and interdependence. Highly individualist cultures believe individual is most important unit. Highly collectivistic cultures believe group is most important unit.

4.1.2　Uncertainty Avoidance

In cross-cultural psychology, uncertainty avoidance is a society's tolerance for uncertainty and ambiguity. It reflects the extent to which members of a society attempt to cope with anxiety by minimizing uncertainty. Uncertainty avoidance is one of five key qualities or dimensions measured by the researchers who developed the Hofstede model of cultural dimensions to quantify cultural differences across international lines and better understand why some ideas and business practices work better in some countries than in others. According to the theory's framework, the dimensions are only applicable to a society as a whole, not for each individual in the society.

4.1.3 Power Distance

Power distance is the extent to which the lower ranking individuals of a society "accept and expect that power is distributed unequally". It is primarily used in psychological and sociological studies on societal management of inequalities between individuals, and individual's perceptions of that management. People in societies with a high power distance are more likely to conform to a hierarchy where "everybody has a place and which needs no further justification". In societies with a low power distance, individuals tend to try to distribute power equally. In such societies, inequalities of power among people would require additional justification.

4.1.4 Masculinity—Femininity

This dimension focuses on how extent to which a society stress achievement or nurture. Masculinity is seen to be the trait which emphasizes ambition, acquisition of wealth, and differentiated gender roles. Femininity is seen to be the trait which stresses caring and nurturing behaviors, sexuality equality, environmental awareness, and more fluid gender roles.

4.1.5 Long-term Orientation

Long-Term Orientation is the fifth dimension of Hofstede which was added after the original four to try to distinguish the difference in thinking between the East and West. From the original IBM studies, this difference was something that could not be deduced. Therefore, Hofstede created a Chinese value survey which was distributed across 23 countries. From these results, and with an understanding of the influence of the teaching of Confucius on the East, long term vs. short term orientation became the fifth cultural dimension.

4.1.6 Indulgence vs. Restraint (Ind)

Indulgence stands for a society that allows relatively free gratification of basic and natural human drives related to enjoying life and having fun. Restraint stands for a society that suppresses gratification of needs and regulates it by means of strict social norms. Hofstede's work established a major research tradition in cross-cultural psychology and has also been drawn upon by researchers and consultants in many fields relating to international business and communication. The theory has been widely used in several fields as a paradigm for research, particularly in cross-cultural psychology, international management, and cross-cultural communication. It continues to be a major resource in cross-cultural fields. It has inspired a number of other major cross-cultural studies of values, as well as research on other aspects of culture, such as social beliefs.

- **case one**

When President George Bush went to Japan with leading American businessmen, he made explicit and direct demands on Japanese leaders, which violated Japanese etiquette. To the Japanese, it is rude and a sign of ignorance or desperation to make direct demands. Some analysts believe it severely damaged the negotiations and confirmed to the Japanese that Americans are barbarians.

- **case two**

A Japanese manager in an American company was told to give critical feedback to subordinate during a performance evaluation. Because the Japanese are used to high context language and uncomfortable with giving direct feedback, it took the manager five tries before he was direct enough for the American subordinate to understand.

4.2　The Challenge of Globalization

Globalization is the international integration of intercultural ideas, perspectives, products/services, culture, and technology. Globalization is a hot topic in the business world today, garnering enormous attention as imports and exports continue to rise with companies expanding across the global marketplace. Understanding the basic overview of the global economy underlines highly relevant managerial and business level applications that provide useful insights to modern-day managers.

In general terms, globalization is the international integration of intercultural ideas, perspectives, products/services, culture, and technology. This has resulted in large scale interdependence between countries, as specialization (arguably the root cause of globalization) allows for specific regions to leverage their natural resources and abilities to efficiently produce specific products/services with which to trade for another country's specialization. This allows for a higher standard of living across the globe through higher efficiency, lower costs, better quality, and a more innovative and dynamic workforce.

4.2.1　Growth of Globalization

The ease of modern globalization is often attributed to rapid technological developments in transportation and communication. These form the central system of international exchange, allowing businesses to create meaningful relationships worldwide with minimal time investment and costs. Management is tasked with ensuring these resources are available to employees and properly leveraged to optimize the geographic reach of a business's operations.

This has led to the existence of many multinational enterprises (MNEs), who argue that survival in the newly globalized economy requires sourcing of raw materials, services, production, and labor.

From a managerial perspective, the global workplace implies an enormous amount of diversity management. Estimates of the world labor pool in 2005 noted that multinational companies employed a stunning 3 billion workers cumulatively, which is nearly half of the entire world population. As a manager, this means developing a globally aware perspective that lends itself well to the specific geographic needs, values, and customs in which the business operates. Developing this global skill set is a powerful managerial skill.

4.2.2   Challenges of Globalization

Managers should also be aware of the best way to approach global demographics from a business to consumer perspective, taking an international product or service and localizing it successfully. This is a significant challenge, necessitating consideration for different tastes and branding strategies during the implementation process. The process of moving from an international product to a localized product happens step by step and the elements of production that can be universally applied have to be compared to those that need a localized touch. A globalizing organization must place an international focus on product design, development, and QA to ensure its broad relevance while also localizing marketing to tailor its appeal to individual markets.

Managers must also be particularly aware of the current criticisms of a highly global society, particularly as it pertains to ethical and environmental considerations. A global economy is, in many ways, enforcing a global culture. This global culture is often criticized for taking the place of previously established domestic cultures (and motivating consumerism). As a result, managers should carefully consider how to best localize products to retain cultural identity in the regions they operate. Environmental concerns are of large importance as well, as the constant energy utilization required for this interchange pollutes the environment and uses high quantities of valuable energy-creating resources. Minimizing the damage done to the environment, and offsetting it as best as possible through philanthropic giving, is not only a wise marketing move but also a critical ethical consideration.

Combining these points, the globalized society presents enormous opportunity for businesses. Intercultural marketplaces allow for differing demographics, larger market potential, a more diverse customer base (and therefore more diverse product offering) and a highly valuable human resource potential. On the other end of the bargain, managers are tasked with localizing products and services effectively in a way that minimizes the adverse cultural and environmental effects caused by this rapid global expansion to maintain an ethical operation.

4.3　Pre-watching Activities

Video One: All the Backstory for "Avengers: Age of Ultron" in 7 Minutes

★ **New Words**

ultron 澳创(美国漫威漫画旗下超级反派)	libido 生命力
lead up 引入；抢先	hyper 亢奋的, 高度紧张的
mega 宏大的	blockbuster 轰动；大片
butler 管家	prick 刺伤, 刺痛
a.k.a. 亦称，又名	wimpy 懦弱的；无用的
hygiene 清洁，卫生	mind bender 扭转思想的人或物
planetoid 小行星	tassel 大战
scrawny 骨瘦如柴的	weakling 虚弱的人
legit 合法的	splinter hydra 九头蛇
blister 水泡	squalling 哭哭啼啼的
vet 老兵	disgraced 失宠的
sequel 续集	covert 隐蔽的

4.3.1　Compound Dictation One

Avenger's age of ultron is the 11th movie set in the so called Marvel cinematic universe. That shared universe also include: 62 television episodes, 31 comic book titles and five DVD only short films. Holy living … is that there is a lot of lead up, but don't worry, we'll tell you all this stuff you actually need to know to be ready for this latest hyper mega super ultra____1____.

It all began in the first iron man movie where we meet Tony Stark, a weapon's designer with a raging libido and a computer butler named Jarvis._____2_____. After getting captured and gravely injured by terrorists in Afghanistan, he builds a robot suit out of a spare parts and returns to the US. He decides he doesn't like weapons manufacturing, builds a better version of his suit, saves southern California from another guy in a robot suit and _____3_____. Right after that, he's approached by a guy named Nick Fury who runs a covert military operation called SHIELD. He says there are secret superheroes around the world and he's putting together a team of them. What will they be avenging? Who knows? But they have another recruit in mind. Bruce Banner a.k.a, the incredible hulk, whom we meet in…well The Incredible Hulk. _____4_____.

_____5_____ After some explosiony hygienes, Bruce goes into hiding and learns to control his powers through meditations and stuff. Don't worry too much about Iron Man 2. The only things to know about it are that _____6_____. He meets a SHILED super spy named Natasha Rimanov, a.k.a. black widow. And he has a complicated relationship with a military dude named James Rhodes. Rhody is a long time friend but thinks Tony needs to cooperate more with the government. He also has some of his own robot armor. They call him War Machine, but it's not nearly as colorful. Then we got the first Thor movie, hoo boy this one is a mind   bender. We meet Thor, a warrior prince from an extra dimensional planetoid called Azgard, which is populated by near immortal beings who used to visit earth. When Oden time, humans thought of them as gods. Thor is very strong. _____ _____7_____. He has an evil brother named Loki. He has a scientist love interest in Jane. And he is aided by the helpful god Hamdo. Thor and Loki get into a Titanic tassel and Thor wins. He encountered a SHILED agent called Clinton Barton a.k.a. hawk guy who only uses bows and arrows for some reason. We also meet a good guy astrophysicist named   Erik Selvic who get secret mind controlled by Loki before Nick Fury recruited him to work for SHILD. Captain America the first avenger is a flash back but a very important one.Meet Steve Rogers a scrawny weakling in the 1940s who volunteers for a military experiment that _____8_____ made of ultra rare mineral Vibranium. After spending some time entertaining audiences as a propaganda tool named Captain America, he becomes a legit soldier doing secret missions against the science obsessed Nazi splinter group called hydra. He stops a big evil hydra plan but seemingly dies while crash landing into some very cold snow. This is very sad for his war buddy and sorta girl friend Peggy Carter. But fear not, we find out that he just got frozen and was discovered in the present where he's sought out and recruited by … you guessed it! Nick Fury! You know what that means. It's time for the first avengers movie!

Loki comes to earth with a super powered soul controlling staff, steals a magic cube and uses it to launch a plan for world domination. Nick Fury rounds up all the super heroes we've already met, sensitive Steve, cool Clint, total dick Tony, thunderous Thor and nasty Natasha who sent to recruit blister out Bruce. They become SHILD'S first, last and only line of defense against Loki's extra dimensional invaders. They become…the avengers! After some squalling and mind control, sorry Hawk guy, _____9_____ in New York City where Iron Man fights a big fat space snake! Then they get some shawarma, hmmm, shawarma. Oh one quick thing, we also learn that Natasha used to work for the Russians but doesn't anymore. You can basically ignore Iron Man Three except you should know that Tony creates a bunch of remote controlled robot suits he calls the Iron Legion and meanwhile entrusts his company to capable girlfriend Pepper Props. And you can mostly ignore Thor, the dark world, aside from one notable item that pros up, a powerful space goo called the ether. This thing holds one of the six infinity stones, back in the avengers Loki had two other infinity stones. And an evil space lord named Fanos wanted to collect them all. Ok enough weird space mystical stuff. Let's talk about Captain America, the winter soldier. _____10_____. But SHIELD is up to some questionable business. They're building a world wide monitoring system that can kill basically everybody. Nick Fury seems fine with this plan until he is attacked and framed as a traitor and it turns out SHIELD has been taken over by… HYDRA. Cap goes on a run with Natasha and his new friend Falcon who is a war vet with a flying machine. They link up with a SHIELD officer named Maria Hill and the disgraced Nick Fury who has faked his own death to go undercover. _____ 11 _____. The world's governments decide to force it to disband, so bye bye SHIELD. You can mostly ignore Guardians of the Galaxy because as fun as it is, it takes place like a bijulion miles away in space and has no avengers in it. The only thing you need to know is that another infinity stones popped up in that one and Thanos really wanted it. Ok, last thing I promise, we have briefly met a pair of twins named Pietro and Wonda Maximoff. According to an obscure tie in comic they're angry activists from a war torn European country called Sokovia. They want to over throw their shitty government. So they volunteer for a Hydra program run by a dude named Baron Struker. The program gave them super powers, so now Pieto can run really fast and Wonda can do weird stuff with her mind. We see them at a short scene at the end of Winter Soldier imprisoned by Hydra and not looking happy about it. And now you are ready to see Avengers: Age of Ultron, which will have approximately 8000 characters, 4 million different locations and 12 billion sequels. Here's hoping our brains don't melt.

4.3.2　Conversation Practice

1. What do all the superheroes in Marvel cinematic universe have in common?
2. Who are the Chinese equivalents of these Marvel superheroes?
3. Who is your superhero in reality?

4.4　Watching Activities

Video Two: The US Sub-prime Crisis

★ New Words

sub-prime crisis 次贷危机	deficit 赤字
bond 债券	mortgage 抵押
Catch 22 第二十二条军规	default 违约

4.4.1　Compound Dictation Two

Meet Uncle Sam. He has a lot of bills to pay, almost $ 4 trillion worth every year. Uncle Sam's income is a little over $ 2 trillion per year. To make up the difference, the deficit, he does what most Americans do. He borrows money. When Uncle Sam takes out a loan, he calls it a bond. Bonds can be held by banks, investors or even foreign governments. _____ 1 _____. Ever think about paying your mortgage with your credit card? That's exactly what Uncle Sam does. He takes out new loans, new bonds, so that he can make payments on the old ones. All those loans and especially all that interest adds up. Right now, Uncle Sam owes about $14 trillion. To put that in perspective, $14 trillion is about the same as the national GDP, the total value of all the goods and services produced by the American economy in an entire year. _____

_____2_____. And he's having trouble just paying the interest on his loans. The obvious solution would be to either cut spending or increase taxes. But if he cuts spending, the people that he's spending money on would complain that they don't have money to spend and that he was hurting the economy. If he tries to raise taxes enough to close this gap, not only would people definitely have less money to spend, he'd probably have riots on his hands. So Uncle Sam chooses the easy way to make money. Just make it. He calls up the Federal Reserve, which is our central bank and like magic, dollars are created and deposited in banks all around America. The problem is if there are more of something there is, the less it's worth.

3_____. That's why commodities like gasoline, food and gold become more expensive when Uncle Sam does his money-making magic. The commodities aren't really worth more; your money is just worth less. That's called inflation. Remember the foreign governments that lent money to Uncle Sam? When they lent money to the American government, something interesting happened. It made the U.S. look richer, and their countries looked poorer. When a country looks poorer compared to America, one dollar of our money buys a lot of their money, so they can pay their workers only a few pennies a day. With such low labor costs, they can sell their products in America for lower prices than any American manufacturer can. The easiest way for American companies to compete is _____4_____.

Americans lose their jobs, stop paying taxes, and start collecting government benefits like Medicaid and unemployment. This means that Uncle Sam has even less income and even more expenses. At the same time, the people who still have jobs are desperate to keep them, so they tend to do more work but not to get paid any more. _____5_____.

And this is why Uncle Sam is in a Catch 22. He can't raise taxes or cut spending without making the recession worse. And he can't have the Federal Reserve create more money without making inflation worse. For now, he can keep borrowing more money but since he can't even pay the interest on the loans he already has, it just makes his inevitable bankruptcy even worse. Whether it's in two months or two years, the day will come when Uncle Sam can no longer pay his bills. When that happens, _____6_____. You see, just like Uncle Sam, governments, banks, and corporations don't actually have much money. Mostly, all they have is debt to each other. _____7_____. If investors can't pay their bills, corporations won't be able to pay their employees. If banks can't pay their bills, you won't be able to take out loan, use a credit card or even withdraw your savings. _____

_____8_____ . _____9_____.

It's never happened before, so nobody really knows how bad it will be, how long it will last, or even how we'll eventually get out of it. The house of cards has already been built. There's no painless way to dismantle it now. All we can do is to educate each other about what's actually going on and to prepare for what may be very extraordinary circumstances.

4.4.2　Oral Practice—Debate

1. How would the US sub-prime crisis affect the global financial market?

2. What's your understanding of the sentence "The house of cards has already been built. There's no painless way to dismantle it now. All we can do is to educate each other about what's actually going on and to prepare for what may be very extraordinary circumstances."?

3. Like it or not, the world is heading for globalization. Some people say globalization does more good than harm to China's economy, but some others hold the opposite. What do you think of it? Please illustrate your arguments.

4.5　Oral Enhancement Drills

4.5.1　Warming Up: Retelling Jokes

❖ **Retell the following joke in your own words:**

A blonde walks into a shop, and finds a sales assistant. She asks, "How much does that TV cost?" But the sales assistant says, "Sorry, we don't sell to blondes". The blonde is disappointed, and leaves the shop. But then she has an idea: she'll change the colour of her hair. So she dyes it brown, goes back to the shop the next day, and finds a different sales assistant. She asks again, "How much does that TV cost?" but that sales assistant also says, "Sorry, we don't sell to blondes". The blonde is surprised, and asks, "But how did you know I was a blonde." The sales assistant says: "Because that's not a TV, that's a microwave."

4.5.2　Cultural Introduction

❖ **Background Information**

Western people don't readily give money to others or receive other's readily. If you lend money to a westerner generously, and said, "Don't mention it again. You don't have to pay me back." he would be angry and think you were looking down on him, not believing his ability to repay the money.

❖ **Ask your partner the following questions:**

1. Have you ever lend or borrow money to or from friend? On what occasions did you lend or borrow the money?

2. What are the common reasons for people to borrow money?

3. Have you ever refused to lend money? Tell the story.

4. If your friends forget to return your money in time, would you remind them?

5. How would you feel if your friends ask for their money back when you forget to return money to them?

❖ **Making up dialogues by using the information given below:**

1. Your friend Carl looks very upset because an unexpected expense comes up and he needs to borrow money from you.

2. Your friend Carl wants to return the money he borrowed from you, you say to him that there's no hurry and he takes it seriously.

❖ **Discussions:**

1. Why do you think the westerners are reluctant to borrow and lend money from friends while we Chinese would prefer the opposite?

2. What do you think of giving cash as a gift?

4.5.3   Free Talk

1. What would you do with the money if you won a lottery of 1 million?
2. What are the advantages and disadvantages of having a lot of money?

4.6   After-class Activities

4.6.1   Cultural Understanding

Video Appreciation. How Pig Parts Make the World Turn

1. How many kinds of products are made of the pigs according to this lecture? What are they?

2. In which country is each kind of products made?

4.6.2   Cultural Listening Comprehension

◈ **Section A**

Directions: In this section, you will hear two long conversations. At the end of each conversation, you will hear four questions. Both the conversation and the questions will be spoken only once. After you hear a question, you must choose the best answer from the four choices marked A), B),C) and D).

· **Conversation One**

Questions 1 to 4 are based on the conversation you have just heard.

1. A) Project organizer.

B) Public relations officer

C) Marketing manager.

D) Market research consultant.

2. A) Quantitative advertising research.

  B) Questionnaire design.

  C) Research methodology.

  D) Interviewer training.

3. A) They are intensive studies of people's spending habits.

  B) They examine relations between producers and customers.

  C) They look for new and effective ways to promote products.

  D) They study trends or customer satisfaction over a long period.

4. A) The lack of promotion opportunity.

  B) Checking charts and tables.

  C) Designing questionnaires.

  D) The persistent intensity.

- **Conversation Two**

Questions 5 to 8 are based on the conversation you have just heard.

5. A) His view on Canadian universities.

  B) His understanding of higher education.

  C) His suggestions for improvements in higher education.

  D) His complaint about bureaucracy in American universities.

6. A) It is well designed.

  B) It is rather inflexible.

  C) It varies among universities.

  D) It has undergone great changes.

7. A) The United States and Canada can learn from each other.

  B) Public universities are often superior to private universities.

  C) Everyone should be given equal access to higher education.

  D) Private schools work more efficiently than public institutions.

8. A) University systems vary from country to country.

  B) Efficiency is essential to university management.

  C) It is hard to say which is better, a public university or a private one.

  D) Many private university in the U.S. are actually large bureaucracies.

◇ **Section B**

Directions: In this section, you will hear two passages. At the end of each passage, you will hear three or four questions. Both the passage and the questions will be spoken only once. After you hear a question, you must choose the best answer from the four choices marked A), B), C) and D).

- **Passage One**

Questions 9 to 11 are based on the passage you have just heard.

9. A) Government's role in resolving an economic crisis.

   B) The worsening real wage situation around the world.

   C) Indications of economic recovery in the United States.

   D) The impact of the current economic crisis on peopled life.

10. A) They will feel less pressure to raise employees' wages.

    B) They will feel free to choose the most suitable employees.

    C) They will feel inclined to expand their business operations.

    D) They will feel more confident in competing with their rivals.

11. A) Employees and companies cooperate to pull through the economic crisis.

    B) Government and companies join hands to create jobs for the unemployed.

    C) Employees work shorter hours to avoid layoffs.

    D) Team work will be encouraged in companies.

- **Passage Two**

Questions 12 to 15 are based on the passage you have just heard.

12. A) Whether memory supplements work.

    B) Whether herbal medicine works wonders.

    C) Whether exercise enhances one's memory.

    D) Whether a magic memory promises success.

13. A) They help the elderly more than the young.

    B) They are beneficial in one way or another.

    C) They generally do not have side effects.

    D) They are not based on real science.

14. A) They are available at most country fairs.

    B) They are taken in relatively high dosage.

    C) They are collected or grown by farmers.

    D) They are prescribed by trained practitioners.

15. A) They have often proved to be as helpful as doing mental exercise.

    B) Taking them with other medications might entail unnecessary risks.

    C) Their effect lasts only a short time.

    D) Many have benefited from them.

◇ **Section C**

Directions: In this section, you will hear three recordings of lectures or talks followed by three or four questions. The recordings will be played only once. After you hear a question, you must choose the best answer from the four choices marked A), B), C) and D).

- **Recording One**

Questions 16 to 18 are based on the recording you have just heard.

16. A) How catastrophic natural disasters turn out to be to developing nations.

　　B) How the World Meteorological Organization studies natural disasters.

　　C) How powerless humans appear to be in face of natural disasters.

　　D) How the negative impacts of natural disasters can be reduced.

17. A) By training rescue teams for emergencies.

　　B) By taking steps to prepare people for them.

　　C) By changing people's views of nature.

　　D) By relocating people to safer places.

18. A) How preventive action can reduce the loss of life.

　　B) How courageous Cubans are in face of disasters.

　　C) How Cubans suffer from tropical storms.

　　D) How destructive tropical storms can be.

- **Recording Two**

Questions 19 to 22 are based on the recording you have just heard.

19. A) Pay back their loans to the American government.

　　B) Provide loans to those in severe financial difficulty.

　　C) Contribute more to the goal of a wider recovery.

　　D) Speed up their recovery from the housing bubble.

20. A) Some banks may have to merge with others.

　　B) Many smaller regional banks are going to fail.

　　C) It will be hard for banks to provide more loans.

　　D) Many banks will have to lay off some employees.

21. A) It will work closely with the government.

　　B) It will endeavor to write off bad loans.

　　C) It will try to lower the interest rate.

　　D) It will try to provide more loans.

22. A) It won't help the American economy to turn around.

　　B) It won't do any good to the major commercial banks.

　　C) It will win the approval of the Obama administration.

　　D) It will not be necessary if the economy starts to shrink again.

- **Recording Three**

Questions 23 to 25 are based on the recording you have just heard.

23. A) Being unable to learn new things.

B) Being rather slow to make changes.

C) Losing temper more and more often.

D) Losing the ability to get on with others.

24. A) Cognitive stimulation.

B) Community activity.

C) Balanced diet.

D) Fresh air.

25. A) Ignoring the signs and symptoms of aging.

B) Adopting an optimistic attitude towards life.

C) Endeavoring to give up unhealthy lifestyles.

D) Seeking advice from doctors from time to time.

Chapter 5　Contexts of Intercultural Communication

5.1　The Importance of Intercultural Communication

Intercultural communication is a discipline that studies communication across different cultures and social groups, or how culture affects communication. Proper intercultural communication studies situations where people from different cultural backgrounds interact and it seeks to understand how people from different countries and cultures act, communicate and perceive the world around them.

With the rapid development of economy of China, the globalization process is forcing businesses in every field to further think and change their strategies in the competition and cooperation of the whole world. Intercultural communication and cross-culture skills play an ever larger role in global strategies. Future elite in what field must acquire effective intercultural competence. Intercultural communication serves a vital role in that it can avoid miscommunication, prevent misunderstandings, and avert mistakes.

5.2　Body Language of Intercultural Communication

As the trend of globalization is strengthened step by step, we may encounter various international communications in our daily life. Except the verbal communication, body language is frequently used and people have realized the significance of body language in intercultural communication. Research shows that when people meet someone for the first time, only 7% of their initial impact on others is determined by the content of what they say while the other 93% of their message is made up of body language (55%) and the tone of their voice (38%).

According to estimates, human body can make out more than 270,000 kinds of posture and movement. This is far more than the sound made out by human body. These postures and movements' meaning are very complex. Sometimes they are definite and material while sometimes they are general and blurry. Some gestures are used to communicate while in some other occasion they are used to self-express.

As the necessary communication tool, body language has important function in intercultural communication. Bradford J. Hall (2002) summarized the main function of body language:

1) Repetition: Body language can reinforce the verbal language by repeating the verbal message nonverbally, such as using a gesture to help the receiver understand the message easily.

2) Substitution: Body language can be used to replace some verbal language to deliver a certain meaning. A hug may be more powerful than any soothing words when you want to comfort your friend.

3) Contradiction: Body language sometimes can betray the speaker by sending contradictory message to the verbal language. For example, we can't keep our face from blushing even say we don't be nervous or we can't slow down our heartbeat if we are scared. So the body language is more reliable than the verbal language sometimes.

4) Accentuation: It can enforce the power when you add a body language with your talk than only use verbal language. When you apologize to someone with a facial expression of apology it will make your apology more convincing.

5) Regulation: The body language also helps us to control the situation of our talking. For example, if a teacher wants his / her students to be quiet, he / she can put the finger on his / her lip.

5.2.1   Intercultural Communication Case One

Take England for example, cultures differ a lot compared to those of our country. In terms of utterances, in order to praise the one who works so hard and is so powerful, Chinese people will say he works like a cow while the English tend to use the phrase "he works like a horse" or "as strong as a horse". To the best of my belief, the reason for that was so simple: In ancient times, Chinese people used cows in cultivation but English people used horses instead. Another example is that English people can call the name of the seniors directly to address them while in China it's considered rude and offensive. In addition, English people address people mostly with "Mr.", "Mrs." or "Ms." together with their family name, no matter who he is or what social status he possesses. However, Chinese people like to address people with both their family name and titles, for example "Director Lee", "Engineer Chen", to show respect. We must be aware of these differences so that we can have better communications with foreigners, otherwise a cultural gap will form.

5.2.2   Intercultural Communication Case Two

When it comes to dealing with privacy, English and Chinese hold different perspectives. English people think private information such as age, marriage, career and so on as something that they should keep to themselves and others do not have the right to interfere with. While with an attempt to greet or to show concerns, Chinese people like to ask others about their family, occupation, etc. and they feel comfortable when being asked such questions because they like to be concerned by others. When hearing words like "You are fat", "You are thin" or "You don't look healthy", English people feel embarrassed. These kinds of words can't express concerns for him or her; rather, they may be interpreted as impoliteness.

5.3　Pre-watching Activities

Video One：Art Expands Horizons

★ New Words

depiction 描绘	transcendence 超越
petal 花瓣	iconic diagram 标志性图示
abolitionists 废奴主义者	atrocities 残酷
trauma 创伤	imbued 使蒙受
harassed 骚扰	reverence 尊敬
lynching 私刑拷打	digress 离题
authenticity 真实性	

5.3.1　Compound Dictation One

As a conceptual artist, _____1_____. I do this through painting, sculpture, video and performance. But regardless of the format, two of my favorite materials are history and dialogue.

In 2007, I created "Lotus," a seven-and-a-half-foot diameter, 600-pound glass depiction of a lotus blossom. In Buddhism, _____2_____. But a closer look at this lotus reveals each petal to be the cross-section of a slave ship. This iconic diagram was taken from a British slaving manual and later used by abolitionists to show the atrocities of slavery. In America, we don't like to talk about slavery, nor do we look at it as a global industry. But by using this Buddhist symbol, I hope to _____3_____ and encourage discussions about our shared past.

To create "Lotus," we carved over 6,000 figures. And this later led to a commission by the City of New York to _____4_____ at the Eagle Academy for Young Men, a school for black and Latino students, the two groups most affected by this history. The same two groups are very affected by a more recent phenomenon, but let me digress.

I've been collecting wooden African figures from tourist shops and flea markets around the world. The authenticity and origin of them is completely debatable, _____5_____. Only recently have I figured out how to use this in my own work.

Since 2012, the world has witnessed the killings of Trayvon Martin, Michael Brown, Eric Garner, Sandra Bland, Tamir Rice and literally countless other unarmed black citizens at the hands of the police, _____6_____. In consideration of these victims and the several times that even I, a law-abiding, Ivy League professor, have been targeted and harassed at gunpoint by the police. I created this body of work simply entitled "BAM."

It was important to erase the identity of each of these figures, to make them all look the same and easier to disregard. To do this, _____7_____. where I resculpted them using bullets. And it was fun, playing with big guns and high-speed video cameras. But my reverence for these figures kept me from actually pulling the trigger, somehow feeling as if I would be shooting myself. Finally, my cameraman, Raul, fired the shots. I then took the fragments of these and created molds, and cast them first in wax, and finally in bronze like the image you see here, _____8_____.

When I showed this work recently in Miami, a woman told me she felt every gun shot to her soul. But she also felt that these artworks memorialized the victims of these killings as well as other victims of racial violence throughout US history.

But "Lotus" and "BAM" are larger than just US history. While showing in Berlin last year, a philosophy student asked me what prompted these recent killings. I showed him a photo of a lynching postcard from the early 1900s and _____9_____. But it's only through questions like his and more thoughtful dialogue about history and race can we evolve as individuals and society.

_____10_____ and an opportunity for people to engage one another in real and necessary conversation.

Thank you.

5.3.2 Conversation Practice

1. By applying history and dialogue, what does the speaker want to do and how does he achieve his goal?

2. How does the speaker depict a lotus blossom and what is the origin of lotus?

3. What is "BAM" and why does the speaker use this word in this passage?

5.4 Watching Activities

Video Two: Three Ways to Fix a Broken News Industry

★ **New Words**

coverage 新闻报道	agenda 议事日程
entrepreneurs 创办人	trench 战壕
industrious 勤奋的	collaborators 合作者
curb 扼制	quarantine 隔离
intimidation 恐吓	mentor 导师
oath 誓言	hysterical 歇斯底里的

5.4.1　Compound Dictation Two

Five years ago, I had my dream job. I was a foreign correspondent in the Middle East reporting for ABC News. But there was a crack in the wall, a problem with our industry that I felt we needed to fix. You see, I got to the Middle East right around the end of 2007, which was just around the midpoint of the Iraq War. But by the time I got there, it was already nearly impossible to find stories about Iraq on air. Coverage had dropped across the board, across networks. And of the stories that did make it, more than 80 percent of them were about us. _____
_____　1　_____.

Afghanistan had already fallen off the agenda. There were less than one percent of all news stories in 2008 that went to the war in Afghanistan. It was the longest war in US history, but information was so scarce that school teachers we spoke to told us they had trouble explaining to their students what we were doing there, when those students had parents who were fighting and sometimes dying overseas.

We had drawn a blank, and it wasn't just Iraq and Afghanistan. _____2_____. And by failing to understand the complex issues of our time, we were facing certain practical implications. How were we going to solve problems that we didn't fundamentally understand, that we couldn't track in real time, and where the people working on the issues were invisible to us and sometimes invisible to each other?

When you look back on Iraq, those years when we were missing the story, were the years when the society was falling apart, when we were setting the conditions for what would become the rise of ISIS, the ISIS takeover of Mosul and terrorist violence that would spread beyond Iraq's borders to the rest of the world.

_____　3　_____. If you were a Middle-East specialist, you knew that Syria was that important from the start. But it ended up being, really, one of the forgotten stories of the Arab Spring. I saw the implications up front. Syria is intimately tied to regional security, to global stability. I felt like we couldn't let that become another one of the stories we left behind.

So I left my big TV job to start a website, called "Syria Deeply." It was designed to be a news and information source that made it easier to understand a complex issue, and for the past four years, it's been a resource for policymakers and professionals working on the conflict in Syria. We built a business model based on consistent, high-quality information, and convening the top minds on the issue. _____4_____. So we started to work our way down the list.

I'm just one of many entrepreneurs, and we are just one of many start-ups trying to fix what's wrong with news. All of us in the trenches know that something is wrong with the news industry. It's broken. Trust in the media has hit an all-time low. And the statistic you're seeing up there is from September — it's arguably gotten worse. But we can fix this. We can fix the news. I know that that's true. You can call me an idealist; I call myself an industrious optimist. And I know there are a lot of us out there. _____5_____.

Idea number one: we need news that's built on deep-domain knowledge. Given the waves and waves of layoffs at newsrooms across the country, we've lost the art of specialization. Beat reporting is an endangered thing. When it comes to foreign news, the way we can fix that is by working with more local journalists, treating them like our partners and collaborators, not just fixers who fetch us phone numbers and sound bites. Our local reporters in Syria and across Africa and across Asia bring us stories that we certainly would not have found on our own. _____6_____. Or this one from Sierra Leone, about a local chief who curbed the spread of Ebola by self—organizing a quarantine in his district. Or this one from the border of Pakistan, about Afghan refugees being forced to return home before they are ready, under the threat of police intimidation. Our local journalists are our mentors. They teach us something new every day, and they bring us stories that are important for all of us to know.

Idea number two: we need a kind of Hippocratic Oath for the news industry, a pledge to first do no harm. Journalists need to be tough. We need to speak truth to power, but we also need to be responsible. We need to live up to our own ideals, and we need to recognize when what we're doing could potentially harm society, where we lose track of journalism as a public service.

I watched us cover the Ebola crisis. We launched Ebola Deeply. We did our best_____ ._____7_____. Public health experts tell me that actually cost us in human lives, because by sparking more panic and by sometimes getting the facts wrong, we made it harder for people to resolve what was actually happening on the ground. All that noise made it harder to make the right decisions.

We can do better as an industry, but it requires us recognizing how we got it wrong last time, and deciding not to go that way next time. It's a choice. We have to resist the temptation to use fear for ratings. And that decision has to be made in the individual newsroom and with the individual news executive. Because the next deadly virus that comes around could be much worse and the consequences much higher, if we do what we did last time; if our reporting isn't responsible and it isn't right.

The third idea? We need to embrace complexity if we want to make sense of a complex world. Embrace complexity — not treat the world simplistically, because simple isn't accurate. We live in a complex world. News is adult education._____8_____. If we don't do that, if we pretend there are just simple answers, we're leading everyone off a steep cliff. Understanding complexity is the only way to know the real threats that are around the corner. It's our responsibility to translate those threats and to help you understand what's real, so you can be prepared and know what it takes to be ready for what comes next.

I am an industrious optimist. I do believe we can fix what's broken. We all want to. There are great journalists out there doing great work — we just need new formats. I honestly believe this is a time of reawakening, reimagining what we can do. I believe we can fix what's broken. I know we can fix the news. I know it's worth trying, and I truly believe that in the end, we're going to get this right. Thank you.

5.4.2　Oral Practice—Debate

1. What are the species-level issues?
2. What's the purpose of "Syria Deeply"?
3. What are the three ideas the speaker figure out to make things better?
4. What is the only way to know the real threats that are around the corner?

5.5　Oral Enhancement Drills

5.5.1　Warming Up: Tongue Twisters

A big black bug bit a big black bear, make the big black bear bleed blood.
A box of biscuits, a batch of mixed biscuits.
Black bug's blood.
Betty beat a bit of butter to make a better batter.

5.5.2　Cultural Introduction

❖ **Background Information**

It's quite often that meeting some awkward situations in your daily life. When handling an awkward situation, you are actually communicating with another person with the purpose of solving a problem. Therefore, it is important for you to be honest. Here are a few tips which will help you to smooth over the process.

1. Preparing the ground. Avoid being too direct.
2. Stating the message clearly. Be specific, saying precisely what you want to talk to the other person about.
3. Staying focused. Stick to the problem until it is solved or some kind of agreement is reached.
4. Getting the other person's point of view. Give them space to say what they think and feel. This can help them to be more cooperative when you try to solve the problem.
5. Suggesting a solution.
6. Using polite forms of expression. Avoid saying things too directly.
7. Using fillers such as um, well, I mean, etc. They can help make the speaker sound less confrontational or aggressive.
8. Using modifiers such as a bit, slightly, really, rather, quite, etc. to soften even a very strong message. They can make the speaker sound more polite.

❖ **Discuss and organize ideas:**

Work in pairs. Think of a few real-life situations where it was difficult for you to decide what to do.

Situation1:＿＿＿＿＿＿＿＿＿＿＿＿＿＿＿＿＿＿＿＿＿＿＿＿＿＿＿＿＿＿

Situation2:＿＿＿＿＿＿＿＿＿＿＿＿＿＿＿＿＿＿＿＿＿＿＿＿＿＿＿＿＿＿

Situation3:＿＿＿＿＿＿＿＿＿＿＿＿＿＿＿＿＿＿＿＿＿＿＿＿＿＿＿＿＿＿

Situation4:＿＿＿＿＿＿＿＿＿＿＿＿＿＿＿＿＿＿＿＿＿＿＿＿＿＿＿＿＿＿

❖ **Using the following questions to help you organize a talk to share with your partner:**

1. What was the difficult situation about?

2. When did it happen?

3. What happened leading up to the situation?

4. What was your decision?

5. Why did you decide this way?

6. Do you regret the decision now, or would you do the same again?

5.5.3　Free Talk

1. What do you prefer to do when you face an awkward situation? Do you think it is necessary to say sorry and cope with it in smooth mood?

2. Can you share with your partner some of your awkward situations?

5.6　After-class Activities

5.6.1　Cultural Understanding

Video Appreciation: Body Language

1. What gesture do you usually like to do and what kind of emotions do they expose?

2. How do you explore gestures or facial expressions or other small movements made by other people?

5.6.2　Cultural Listening Comprehension

◇ **Section A**

Directions: In this section, you will hear two long conversations. At the end of each conversation, you will hear some questions. Both the conversation and the questions will be spoken only once. After you hear a question, you must choose the best answer from the four choices marked A), B), C) and D).

- **Conversation One**

Questions 1 to 4 are based on the conversation you have just heard.

1. A) Checking his test score.
   B) Inquiring about a selective course.
   C) Confirming an interview.
   D) Looking for some painting work.

2. A) They dry in a short time.
   B) They are easy to find in stores.
   C) They come in many unusual colors.
   D) They feel pleasant to the touch.

3. A) Complete unfinished projects.
   B) Practice techniques he has learned before.
   C) Teach less advanced students how to use spray paints.
   D) Learn how to apply paints with different kinds of brushes.

4. A) See the woman's work.
   B) Ask his roommate for advice.
   C) Order some supplies.
   D) Sign up for the art class.

- **Conversation Two**

Questions 5 to 8 are based on the conversation you have just heard.

5. A) Sightseeing and eating seafood.
   B) Lying in the sun on the beach.
   C) Taking photos of the plankton.
   D) Doing biological research underwater.

6. A) He was on a field trip.
   B) He was visiting his parents.
   C) He was studying most of the time.
   D) He was on vacation at home.

7. A) They are not large enough to be seen.
   B) They're only freely floating plants.
   C) Jellyfish is a kind of plankton.
   D) All the plankton has transparent tissues.

8. A) They are too small to the eyes.
   B) They move very quickly.
   C) They are transparent.
   D) They are rarely found near the surface.

◇ **Section B**

Directions: In this section, you will hear two passages. At the end of each passage, you will hear some questions. Both the passage and the questions will be spoken only once. After you hear a question, you must choose the best answer from the four choices marked A), B), C) and D).

- **Passage One**

Questions 9 to 12 are based on the passage you have just heard.

9. A) It was named after a French king.

    B) It was named after a place.

    C) It was named after its inventor.

    D) It was named after a factory.

10. A) By putting sugar rather than sweet.

    B) By human feet stamps.

    C) By simple machines.

    D) By beating with shoes.

11. A) It tastes a little bitter rather than sweet.

    B) It is manufactured in more wine-producing areas.

    C) It is mad of rice instead of grape juice now.

    D) It boasts more varieties and better quality now.

12. A) It causes problems occasionally.

    B) It stands for romance.

    C) It seems to be a kind of life necessity.

    D) It is only for breakfast.

- **Passage Two**

Questions 13 to 15 are based on the passage you have just heard.

13. A) Because Amery Ice Shelf is the largest and most typical ice shelf.

    B) Because they wanted to challenge themselves in extreme climate.

    C) Because they desired to collect stuff to study global warming.

    D) Because they were curious of the living conditions there.

14. A) Taking advantage of rare sunshine.

    B) Putting up with annoying beats.

    C) Having access to nutritious food.

    D) Protecting themselves from coldness.

15. A) Small.

    B) Changing.

    C) Remote.

    D) Unbearable.

◇ Section C

Directions: In this section, you will hear three recordings of lectures or talks followed by some questions. The recordings will be played only once. After you hear a question, you must choose the best answer from the four choices marked A), B), C) and D).

- **Recording One**

Questions 16 to 19 are based on the recording you have just heard.

16. A) They were too old to have kids.

    B) They had great risk of having kids.

    C) Their biological clocks were reset.

    D) They needed more time to have kids.

17. A) They are slightly younger.

    B) They never attend college.

    C) They are financially independent.

    D) They have a partner.

18. A) She was afraid she'd be alone forever.

    B) She wanted to have a perfect family.

    C) She was financially and mentally ready.

    D) She got an offer from a sperm donor.

19. A) It is unacceptable to for unmarried women have kids.

    B) It has bad influence on kids, families, and society.

    C) It is not a decision woman can make easily.

    D) It is a decision of last resort for women.

- **Recording Two**

Questions 20 to 22 are based on the recording you have just heard.

20. A) Health care issues.

    B) Drinking-related crimes.

    C) Property damage.

    D) A loss of worker productivity.

21. A) It is about individuals who drink a glass of beer with dinner.

    B) It concerns people who drink a lot in a long period of time.

    C) It applies to not only the U.S. but also other nations.

    D) It brings different consequences in different countries.

22. A) She died at a relative old age.

    B) She died due to excessive drinking.

    C) She died as a result of drunk driving.

    D) She died because of using drugs.

- **Recording Three**

Questions 23 to 25 are based on the recording you have just heard.

23. A) To invest $215 million in free e-Books for students.

B) To make sure every student has access to libraries.

C) To connect all American students to high-speed Internet.

D) To ensure enough money for every single child.

24. A) It provides two-year free education at community colleges.

B) It helps every American receive free high school education.

C) He will talk about it in an opening ceremony next week.

D) It aims to raise the graduation rate by two times in the US.

25. A) It leads to success to our own children.

B) It is equal to a better life for children.

C) It shows kids that their lives are meaningful.

D) It demonstrates our belief in freedom for all.

Chapter 6　Barriers and Bridges Intercultural Communication

6.1　Identifying Cultural Difference

According to Wikipedia, cultural difference is also named as cultural diversity, which is the quality of diverse or different cultures, as opposed to monoculture, the global monoculture, or a homogenization of cultures, akin to cultural decay. The phrase cultural diversity can also refer to having different cultures respect each other's differences. The phrase "cultural diversity" is also sometimes used to mean the variety of human societies or cultures in a specific region, or in the world as a whole. Globalization is often said to have a negative effect on the world's cultural diversity.

Cultural difference arises due to a variety of factors. Individual differences in goals, expectations, values, proposed courses of action, and suggestions about how to best handle a situation, are unavoidable (Darling and Fogliasso 1999). When studying abroad, traveling in a foreign country or just learning a foreign language, we may come across a large number of culture differences. They are so inevitable in all aspects of social life. Without cultural awareness of those differences, embarrassment or misunderstandings will occur.

6.2　Communicating Effectively

In order to communicate effectively, being familiar with different cultures seems necessary. For example, individualism prevails in many western countries. People there are encouraged to develop self-confidence, to speak up or even to show up in public. On the contrary, Chinese people are taught to emphasize collectivism. They are always modest, courtesy and tend to keep silent when they have ideas. These differences in both cultures, which are so obvious, also lead to differences in personalities of Westerners and Chinese. As the saying goes, when in Rome, do as the Romans do. Therefore, it's better to wipe off the habit of being modest and express your ideas bravely.

Cultural differences should be paid more attention to and we need a good grasp of those differences so that we can live in an unfamiliar environment much easily. Besides, in the process of getting more and more information about the cultural differences, we must put our knowledge into practice.

6.3　Pre-watching Activities

Video One：A Visual History of Social Dance in 25 Moves

★ New Words

choreographed 编舞	bubble up 冒出，涌现
enslaved 被奴役的	plantation 种植园
stripped of 被剥夺	shuffle 曳步舞，拖着脚走
improvising 即兴创作	subversive 颠覆性的
parodied 滑稽的模仿	shade 背影
musicality 乐感	permeated 渗透，弥漫

6.3.1　Compound Dictation One

This is the Bop. The Bop is a type of social dance.

Dance is a language, and social dance is an expression that emerges from a community. A social dance isn't choreographed by any one person. It can't be traced to any one moment.

_____1_____.

Because of that, social dances bubble up, they change and they spread like wildfire.

They are as old as our remembered history. In African-American social dances, we see over 200 years of how African and African-American traditions influenced our history.

_____2_____.

The Juba dance was born from enslaved Africans' experience on the plantation. Brought to the Americas, stripped of a common spoken language, _____3_____. It may have looked something like this.

Slapping thighs, shuffling feet and patting hands: this was how they got around the slave owners' ban on drumming, improvising complex rhythms just like ancestors did with drums in Haiti or in the Yoruba communities of West Africa._____4_____.

It was the same subversive spirit that created this dance: the Cakewalk, a dance that parodied the mannerisms of Southern high society -_____5_____. The crazy thing about this dance is that the Cakewalk was performed for the masters, who never suspected they were being made fun of.

Now you might recognize this one, 1920s — the Charleston. The Charleston was all about improvisation and musicality, making its way into Lindy Hop, _____6_____ and even the Kid n Play, originally called the Funky Charleston.

Started by a tight-knit Black community near Charleston, South Carolina, the Charleston permeated dance halls where young women suddenly _____7_____.

Now, social dance is about community and connection; _____8_____. But what if it becomes a worldwide craze? Enter the Twist. It's no surprise that the Twist can be traced back to the 19th century, brought to America from the Congo during slavery. But in the late'50s, right before the Civil Rights Movement, the Twist is popularized by Chubby Checker and Dick Clark. Suddenly, everybody's doing the Twist: white teenagers, kids in Latin America, making its way into songs and movies. ﹒_____9_____.

The story continues in the 1980s and'90s. Along with the emergence of hip-hop, African-American social dance took on even more visibility, borrowing from its long past, shaping culture and being shaped by it.

Today, these dances continue to evolve, grow and spread.

Why do we dance? To move, to let loose, to express. Why do we dance together? To heal, to remember, to say: "We speak a common language. We exist and we are free."

6.3.2　Conversation Practice

1. What is dance is about? And what's the relationship between dance and history?
2. How many dances are introduced in the passage and what do they represent?
3. Are dance steps very important? And do they have potential meanings?

6.4　Watching Activities

Video Two: The Playful Wonderland behind Great Inventions

★ New Words

mammoth 猛犸象	griffon vulture 秃头鹫
vicinity 邻近地区	dispersed 分散
flute 长笛	preposterous 荒唐的
molecules 分子	frivolous 轻率的
momentous 关键的，重大的	trajectories 弹道，轨迹
levers 杠杆	clavichords 翼琴
harpsichords 大键琴	cylinder 圆筒，圆柱，气缸
Parisian elite 巴黎上层精英	

6.4.1 Compound Dictation Two

Roughly 43,000 years ago, a young cave bear died in the rolling hills on the northwest border of modern day Slovenia. A thousand years later, a mammoth died in southern Germany. A few centuries after that, a griffon vulture also died in the same vicinity. And we know almost nothing about how these animals met their deaths, but these different creatures dispersed across both time and space did share one remarkable fate. _____ _____1_____.

Think about that for a second. Imagine you're a caveman, 40,000 years ago. You've mastered fire. You've built simple tools for hunting. You've learned how to craft garments from animal skins to keep yourself warm in the winter. What would you choose to invent next? It seems preposterous that you would invent the flute, a tool that created useless vibrations in air molecules. _____2_____.

Now this turns out to be surprisingly common in the history of innovation. Sometimes people invent things because they want to stay alive or feed their children or conquer the village next door. But just as often, _____3_____. And here's the really strange thing: many of those playful but seemingly frivolous inventions ended up sparking momentous transformations in science, in politics and society.

Take what may be the most important invention of modern times: programmable computers. Now, the standard story is that computers descend from military technology, since many of the early computers were designed specifically to crack wartime codes or calculate rocket trajectories. _____4_____.
The idea behind the flute, of just pushing air through tubes to make a sound, was eventually modified to create the first organ more than 2,000 years ago. Someone came up with the brilliant idea of triggering sounds by pressing small levers with our fingers, inventing the first musical keyboard. Now, keyboards evolved from organs to clavichords to harpsichords to the piano, until the middle of the 19th century, _____5_____.
In fact, the very first typewriter was originally called "the writing harpsichord."

Flutes and music led to even more powerful breakthroughs. About a thousand years ago, at the height of the Islamic Renaissance, three brothers in Baghdad designed a device that was an automated organ. They called it "the instrument that plays itself." Now, the instrument was basically a giant music box. The organ could be trained to play various songs by using instructions encoded by placing pins on a rotating cylinder. And if you wanted the machine to play a different song, you just swapped a new cylinder in with a different code on it. This instrument was the first of its kind. It was programmable.

Now, conceptually, this was a massive leap forward. _____ _____6_____. And that incredibly powerful concept didn't come to us as an instrument of war or of conquest, or necessity at all. It came from the strange delight of watching a machine play music.

In fact, the idea of programmable machines was exclusively kept alive by music for about 700 years. In the 1700s, music-making machines became the playthings of the Parisian elite. Showmen used the same coded cylinders to control the physical movements of what were called automata, an early kind of robot. One of the most famous of those robots was, you guessed it, an automated flute player designed by a brilliant French inventor named Jacques de Vaucanson.

And as de Vaucanson was designing his robot musician, he had another idea. If you could program a machine to make pleasing sounds, _____7_____? Instead of using the pins of the cylinder to represent musical notes, they would represent threads with different colors. If you wanted a new pattern for your fabric, you just programmed a new cylinder. This was the first programmable loom.

Now, the cylinders were too expensive and time-consuming to make, but a half century later, another French inventor named Jacquard hit upon the brilliant idea of using paper-punched cards instead of metal cylinders. _____8_____. That punch card system inspired Victorian inventor Charles Babbage to create his analytical engine, the first true programmable computer ever designed. And punch cards were used by computer programmers as late as the 1970s.

So ask yourself this question: what really made the modern computer possible? Yes, the military involvement is an important part of the story, but inventing a computer also required other building blocks: music boxes, toy robot flute players, harpsichord keyboards, colorful patterns woven into fabric, and that's just a small part of the story. _____9_____: public museums, rubber, probability theory, the insurance business and many more.

Necessity isn't always the mother of invention. The playful state of mind is fundamentally exploratory, seeking out new possibilities in the world around us. And that seeking is why so many experiences that started with simple delight and amusement eventually led us to profound breakthroughs.

_____10_____, but thinking about play and delight this way also helps us detect what's coming next. Think about it: if you were sitting there in 1750 trying to figure out the big changes coming to society in the 19th, the 20th centuries, automated machines, computers, artificial intelligence, a programmable flute entertaining the Parisian elite would have been as powerful a clue as anything else at the time. It seemed like an amusement at best, not useful in any serious way, but it turned out to be the beginning of a tech revolution that would change the world.

You'll find the future wherever people are having the most fun.

6.4.2　Oral Practice—Debate

1. What are the different purposes of human beings to invent things?
2. How many inventions does the speaker mention in this passage and why are these

inventions invented?

3. What really made the modern computer possible?

4. What is the mother of invention?

6.5   Oral Enhancement Drills

6.5.1   Warming Up: Tongue Twisters

Luke Luck likes lakes.

Luke's duck likes lakes.

Luke Luck licks lakes.

Luck's duck licks lakes.

Duck takes licks in lakes Luke Luck likes.

Luke Luck takes licks in lakes duck likes.

6.5.2   Cultural Introduction

❖ **Background Information**

When people receive help from others, they usually show their gratitude by saying "Thank you!", "Thanks!" or "Thanks a lot!". In a more formal situation they many use "I really appreciate this.", or "I'd appreciate that very much." If you want to mention the specific help you have received, you can add it by saying "Thank you for …", " I am grateful for…", or "I just want you to know how much I appreciate your …". The person who is giving help may respond with the words "Think nothing of it.", "Don't mention it.", or simply say "You're welcome." In addition to this, expressions such as "That was really nice of you." and "It was so sweet of you." used by women are suitable choices to say thanks. But if you want to express yourself in a more indirect and delicate way, it is advisable to say "I don't know what I could have done without your help.", or "You shouldn't have gone to any trouble but thank you very much."

If you have done something wrong or have hurt someone, do not hesitate to say, "I'm sorry." or "Excuse me." Sometimes it is necessary to mention what has happened by saying "I'm really sorry that I…" or "Please forgive me for…", which makes your apology more formal. Maybe the trouble is caused by a slip of the tongue or a misunderstanding. In this case, you can clear it up with the expressions "I didn't mean it that way." or "I didn't mean to say …". Of course, it is more likely that you will be forgiven if you are brave enough to show your regret directly by saying "I shouldn't have…".

❖ **Ask the following questions:**

1. What kind of people can teach us important lessons?

2. What is really important in life?

3. To whom should you give and sacrifice?

4. What is necessary for giving and sacrifice?

5. What does giving and sacrifice bring to our life?

❖ **Making up dialogues by using the information given below:**

1. Recall the help you have received from others and something wrong you have done to others.

2. Accept gratitude or apologies.

❖ **Discussions:**

1. What does friendship mean to you? If your good friend did something wrong and it really made you sad, would you be willing to forgive him/her?

2. Should one express his/her gratitude to people who help him/her?

6.5.3　Free Talk

1. What do you do in your spare time?

2. Do you prefer to do something or nothing when you have spare time? Why?

6.6　After-class Activities

6.6.1　Cultural Understanding

Video Appreciation: 4 Reasons to Learn a New Language

1. Why should we learn a new language?

2. What is the purpose of the speaker mentioning the movie by the Canadian film director Denys Armand?

6.6.2　Cultural Listening Comprehension

◈ **Section A**

Directions: In this section, you will hear two long conversations. At the end of each conversation, you will hear some questions. Both the conversation and the questions will be spoken only once. After you hear a question, you must choose the best answer from the four choices marked A), B), C) and D).

· **Conversation One**

Questions 1 to 4 are based on the conversation you have just heard.

1. A) A director of a sales department.

  B) A manager at a computer store.

  C) A sales clerk at a shopping center.

  D) An accountant of a computer firm.

2. A) Handling customer complaints.

  B) Recruiting and training new staff.

  C) Dispatching ordered goods on time.

  D) Developing computer programs.

3. A) She likes something more challenging.

  B) She likes to be nearer to her parents.

  C) She wants to have a better-paid job.

  D) She wants to be with her husband.

4. A) Right away.

  B) In two months.

  C) Early next month.

  D) In a couple of days.

- **Conversation Two**

Questions 5 to 8 are based on the conversation you have just heard.

5. A) It will face challenges unprecedented in its history.

  B) It is a resolute advocate of the anti-global movement.

  C) It is bound to regain its full glory of a hundred years ago.

  D) It will be a major economic power by the mid-21st century.

6. A) The lack of overall urban planning.

  B) The huge gap between the haves and have-nots.

  C) The inadequate supply of water and electricity.

  D) The shortage of hi-tech personnel.

7. A) They attach great importance to education.

  B) They are able to grasp growth opportunities.

  C) They are good at learning from other nations.

  D) They have made use of advanced technologies.

8. A) Neutral.

  B) Pessimistic.

  C) Optimistic.

  D) Anxious.

◇ Section B

Directions: In this section, you will hear two passages. At the end of each passage, you will hear some questions. Both the passage and the questions will be spoken only once. After you hear a question, you must choose the best answer from the four choices marked A), B), C) and D).

- **Passage One**

Questions 9 to 12 are based on the passage you have just heard.

9. A) She taught chemistry and microbiology courses in a college.

   B) She gave lectures on how to become a public speaker.

   C) She helped families move away from industrial polluters.

   D) She engaged in field research on environmental pollution.

10. A) The job restricted her from revealing her findings.

    B) The job posed a potential threat to her health.

    C) She found the working conditions frustrating.

    D) She was offered a better job in a minority community.

11. A) Some giant industrial polluters have gone out of business.

    B) More environmental organizations have appeared.

    C) Many toxic sites in America have been cleaned.

    D) More branches of her company have been set up.

12. A) Her widespread influence among members of Congress.

    B) Her ability to communicate through public speaking.

    C) Her rigorous training in delivering eloquent speeches.

    D) Her lifelong commitment to domestic and global issues.

- **Passage Two**

Questions 13 to 15 are based on the passage you have just heard.

13. A) The fierce competition in the market.

    B) The growing necessity of staff training.

    C) The accelerated pace of globalization.

    D) The urgent need of a diverse workforce.

14. A) Gain a deep understanding of their own culture.

    B) Take courses of foreign languages and cultures.

    C) Share the experiences of people from other cultures.

    D) Participate in international exchange programs.

15. A) Reflective thinking is becoming critical.

    B) The labor market is getting globalized.

    C) Knowing a foreign language is essential.

    D) Globalization will eliminate many jobs.

◇ **Section C**

Directions: In this section, you will hear three recordings of lectures or talks followed by some questions. The recordings will be played only once. After you hear a question, you must choose the best answer from the four choices marked A), B), C) and D).

- **Recording One**

Questions 16 to 19 are based on the recording you have just heard.

16. A) One in three Chinese men will die from smoking.
    B) Two-thirds of all Chinese youngsters are smokers.
    C) Most young male smokers start smoking before 20.
    D) Half of the Chinese men will die from smoking.

17. A) There is a quick solution to solve the problem.
    B) It's too difficult to make the problem go away.
    C) There is no way to reduce deaths from smoking.
    D) Stop smoking is the only solution to the problem.

18. A) The percentage of Chinese female smokers has dropped.
    B) Only one percent of Chinese women die from smoking.
    C) Smoking has been fashionable among Chinese women.
    D) Smoking has made Chinese women more attractive.

19. A) He is the only author of the report on smoking.
    B) He suggests an increase of the cigarette price.
    C) He changes public attitudes about smoking.
    D) He predicts the health effects of smoking.

- **Recording Two**

Questions 20 to 22 are based on the recording you have just heard.

20. A) The country has worked on generating new energy.
    B) People have been asked to lower carbon emissions.
    C) All businesses made commitments to act on climate.
    D) The businesses stepped up only to save the planet.

21. A) 150 countries have reduced their levels of carbon pollutions.
    B) Over 85% of the global emissions have warmed our planet.
    C) Many countries have made plans to control carbon pollution.
    D) It has given a chance to America to go to Paris this December.

22. A) It has contributed greatly to land protection.
    B) It has cost taxpayers money to protect the land.
    C) It has benefited a few states in America.
    D) It has been reauthorized and funded by the congress.

- **Recording Three**

Questions 23 to 25 are based on the recording you have just heard.

23. A) To plan a few minutes after breakfast time.
    B) To have a regular and focused course of study.

C) To get crazy in mastering a language in 30 days.

D) To take small steps when feeling disinterested.

24. A) Visual learners need to see learning models.

B) Auditory learners have to hear instructions.

C) Tactile learners learn through practice.

D) The preferences are determined by cultures.

25. A) They are singular in nature.

B) They are of many dimensions.

C) They can vary from time to time.

D) They are determined by situations.

Chapter 7   American and British Cultural Communication

7.1   Difference between American and British Cultural Communication

There are vast differences in culture between Americans and their British Commonwealth counterparts throughout the world. American English is spoken in the USA, Canada and many Pacific Rim countries where America has exerted an influence. British English is spoken throughout the British Commonwealth of 54 countries, some of the most notable being the United Kingdom, Australia, New Zealand and South Africa, with Canada being the exception. Although part of the Commonwealth, Canadians tend to speak a mixture of American and British English due to that country's proximity to the USA (although they spell the British way). British English and American English differ in terms of spelling, meaning, pronunciation and slang words. They also have differences in driving practices, with Commonwealth countries driving on the left. There are different etiquettes prevalent between the two cultures. In addition, you can find all sorts of miscellaneous differences including measurements, legal driving and drinking ages as well as lifestyle differences like choice of bedding and even how toilets differ!

7.2   Famous Landmark

Visiting famous landmarks is a great way to make history come alive, and not just for history buffs, but for the whole family. Here are just 5 of the top US historical landmarks everyone should visit in their lifetime to experience an unforgettable journey into the past.

1. Thomas Jefferson's Monticello, Charlottesville, Virginia
2. The Lincoln Memorial, Washington D.C.
3. Ellis Island, New York City, New York.
4. Independence Hall, Philadelphia, Pennsylvania.
5. Plimoth Plantation, Plymouth, Massachusetts

From Stonehenge, and Hadrian's wall to grand castles and ancient buildings, Britain has a lot of history waiting to be explored.

1. Stonehenge, Wiltshire
2. Edinburgh Castle, Edinburgh
3. Roman Baths, Bath
4. Windsor Castle, Berkshire
5. Iron bridge Gorge, Shropshire

7.3　Symbols of American and British Culture

American culture is unique, Statue of Liberty, American Gothic, Buffalo Nickel, Uncle Sam and Barbie dolls are five famous symbols of it. Statue of Liberty represents democracy and freedom of American culture. American Gothic represents the pursuit of diligence of American culture. Buffalo Nickel represents the pursuit of pioneering spirit of American culture. Uncle Sam represents the pursuit of patriotism of American culture. Barbie dolls represent the pursuit of women's liberation of American culture. Analysis of five famous symbols of American culture is important for us to know American culture comprehensively.

The top 10 symbols of British culture, which the respondents said they were proud of, are:

1. Shakespeare
2. National Trust and armed forces
3. Union Jack, flag of the United Kingdom
4. The Great Britain Pound
5. National Health Service .
6. The British monarchy
7. BBC
8. Sporting achievements
9. The Beatles and the legal system
10. Parliament

7.4　Pre-watching Activities

Video One: Different Meanings of Words in Britain and America

★ New Words

sprout 壶嘴	aluminium (br.)铝
aluminum (Am.)铝	obese 肥胖的
fictional 虚构的	

7.4.1   Compound Dictation One

Please welcome David Williams and Ben Stiller.

D (David Williams): Good evening. My name is David Williams and I am a British.

B (Ben Stiller): Hi, I'm Ben Stiller and I'm an American. USA USA USA USA!

D: Amnesty International has invited us here this evening to_____1_____.

B: The first word is jugs.

D: In Britain, this is a_____2_____.

B: Tits.

D: Next is hooters. For the British, these are_____3_____.

B: Tits again.

D: Aluminium,_____4_____.

B: Aluminum, a silvery white metal.

D: It's aluMinium.

B:It's aluminum.

D: AluMin- i – u – m

B: Alumin – um

D:-I – u – m

B:-um

D: A la mode, from the French, on the fashion.

B: _____5_____.

D: Passport, an official government document that permits a citizen to travel abroad.

B: We don't have that word in America.

B: Dentist,_____6_____.

D: We don't have that word in Britain.

D: Obese, anyone over 200 pounds.

D: Anyone over 2000 pounds.

D: Blue steel, _____7_____.

D: In America?

D: Piers Morgan, an annoying man who used to be on TV in Britain.

B: _____8_____.

D: Bush, a private part that is too embarrassing to mention.

B: Same in here then.

D: _____9_____, a way of settling scores in soccer.

B: A way of settling scores in Texas.

B: Voice mail, a place where _____10_____.

D: A place where friends or family members leave messages for journalists to listen to later.

D: Harry Potter, _____11_____who goes to Hogwarts School.

B: Fictional?

D: Yeah, of course. Harry Potter is fictional.

B: OK. But the Quidditch thing, that's real, right?

D: No, no, you know, it's made up, _____12_____, like Night in the Museum.

B: Night in the museum isn't real?

D: Our final word tonight is Ass, a donkey.

B: Buttocks/ boody/ junk in the trunk/ bubble/ dookie maker…

D: Yes, thank you. We get the picture.

B: I think you'll agree, my British friend, that we Americans knew Brits really do speak the same language.

D: No, we don't.

B: It's alumin – um

D: Shut up!

7.4.2　Conversation Practice

1. What kind of differences of British and American English does this cross-talk present?
2. Which do you prefer, British English or American English?

7.5　Watching Activities

Video Two: The British and the American

★ New Words

condiment 调味品；佐料	Pound Land 英国最大的廉价商品连锁店
illicit 违法的；不正当的	Channing Tatum 查宁·塔图姆(美国影视演员)
Walmart 沃尔玛（世界连锁零售企业）	complementary 补足的，补充的
Gatorade　佳得乐（一种运动饮料）	pastry 油酥点心；面粉糕饼
bizarre　奇异的（指态度，容貌，款式等）	sappy 愚笨的

7.5.1　Compound Dictation Two

When I came to study abroad in England, I pretty much thought that it would be_____1_____

_____1_____. I mean we both speak the same language basically, but everything else between the English people and the American is _____2_____. And it's not just the fact that they use mint jelly as a condiment or that they drink tea every hour every day. It's the little things, like asking "How are you", for example. In the U.S., when we ask someone how they are we say: "How are you?" In England, it's a little different. They say, "You alright?", which…is weird because in the U.S.

usually when you ask someone if you are alright, _____3_____. So every time someone in England ask me "You alright?" I always have to like three seconds _____4_____, and then I'm very intelligible saying something like "Yeah, I mean…yes. I am alright." "Uh…are you alright?" and then there is a whole knife thing. Since I move here for three months, I went to Poundland and bought kitchen's supplies because I don't really need them last long. But what I didn't expect, when I got to the counter was that the cashier will take out the knife and hold it up as if _____5_____ or something from her. I just remember her looking at me, and then asking for my ID, which she looked at for 20 seconds before she called her manager. So the manager comes over, and he spends a good 30 seconds looking at my picture on my license, comparing it to me. And meanwhile I am standing there, contemplating whether or not I should crush out of the Poundland window like I am Channing Tatum way to house down or something. But I keep it cool, and the manager gives you, ok, I am allowed to purchase the knife. I'm sorry. But if you like U.K., should learn Americans this kind of thing. Because when you grow up in a country where the cashier in Walmart asks _____6_____ in your bag or not, it's alarming to ____7____ for trying to buy _____7_____! Speaking of eating, English people seem to _____8_____. Americans are big fan into walking and drinking. If it's not a cup of cappuccino, it's coke, a Gatorade or maybe even the water stuff that people are talking about. But here in England, it's sandwiches. People in England like sandwiches. It's like no matter where you are and what time it is, someone is walking around eating a sandwich or like these pastry things which basically look like fat hot pocket. Every few feet in England _____9_____. You can even buy sandwiches in the freaking beauty store. But maybe _____10_____. They will run you over. There is about a 0% chance that someone will stop it they see you in the middle of the street even if it is a mother, pushing her baby across the street in a crossroad. A car will literally wait to the last possible second before slamming on their breaks and blowing their honk. Honestly though _____11_____. In the U.S. we drive on the right so technically you're side supposed to walk at the right of the side walk. So you would think that because English people drive on the left, they will walk on the left side of the side walk. You will be wrong. I can now tell you _____12_____ when the person coming towards me, _____12_____. This generally leads to like this awkward "oh, sorry" thing before I have to move to the right to let them pass. But even more strange, if there are a group of people taking up the whole side walk and you are walking towards them, 80% of time they will make no effort what's so ever to let you pass. I felt people almost push me into the oncoming traffic because they are so unwilling to move to the left side of the side walk to let me pass. All I am saying is you make your choice in England. You guys wrote like "Hey guys, let's drive on the left hand side of the road", so left hand side is your side. You can't decide to walk at the right side of the sidewalk. That just… it's not cool. If you want to walk at the right side on the side walk, then the escalator should go the right way and you should drive on the right hand side of the road. (sigh)

Put _____13_____, I really do love here in England. I like the fact that you can go and buy a good sandwich at the drug store and running outdoor, here has pretty much satisfied my urge of ever wanting to run across a Martio car track. So…I think it's a win-win either way. It may be a lot of things I don't understand here, and in two weeks when I leave, there're still gonna be things that I don't understand. But I am very glad that _____14_____. And…that's your happy ending for you. I have nothing else. Cheers!

7.5.2　Oral Practice—Debate

1. What examples does the speaker give about "everything else between the English people and the American is basically completely different."?

2. What attitudes does the speaker hold towards all the differences? How do you understand "But I am very glad that I got a chance to experience them." ?

3. As a Chinese English learner, do you think it is necessary for us to speak standard British or American English or it is ok for us to speak English with Chinese accent?

7.6　Oral Enhancement Drills

7.6.1　Warming Up: Retelling Personal Stories

Think of an interesting story from your life and then write your name and a title for your story on the slip of paper which you give them. Work in pairs, tell each other the story, and then swap the piece of paper. Then when you form a new pair with another person, you will repeat the procedure, telling the story on the slip of paper which you now hold.

7.6.2　Cultural Introduction

❖ **Background Information**

In Western cultures, gifts are often wrapped and accompanied by a gift note. On the card, it would say: Happy Birthday, Happy Anniversary, or Congratulations! depending on the occasion. When visiting someone, it's polite to bring a small gift. And usually it's interesting and exciting to see what's inside the wrapped gift. When it comes to opening gifts, in western culture, you can go either way: Opening the gifts in front of the guests or opening it later in private.

Describe a gift that you recently gave to others. When did it happen? Who you gave it to? What gift you gave to the person? And explain why you gave this gift to others.

❖ **Ask the following questions:**

1. Do you think it's easy to choose what to give other people?

2. What should you consider when choosing a gift?

3. On what occasions would people give gifts?

4. Do you think gift-giving is very important? Why or why not?

5. Would you open the gift you are given in front of the guests? Why or why not?

❖   **Making up dialogues by using the information given below:**

1. At your birthday party, a friend of you gives you a gift and insists on you opening it in his/her presence. However, it turns out to be something a bit personal and you feel a little embarrassed.

2. You are discussing with your colleague what gift to give your boss on her birthday. And you two have different opinions.

❖ **Discussions:**

1. Do you think some parents give too many things to their children?

2. Can you suggest any ways to improve that situation?

7.6.3   Free Talk

1. Do you remember your parents birthday?

2. How do you celebrate it?

3. What is the best gift for parents?

7.7   After-class Activities

7.7.1   Cultural Understanding

Video appreciation : Why I Keep Speaking up, even When People Mock My Accent?

1. What does the speaker mean by saying "I've come to understand that 'normal' has a lot to do with expectations."?

2. Do you have accent problem? Does it bother you? Why or why not?

7.7.2   Cultural Listening Comprehension

◈ **Section A**

Directions: In this section, you will hear 8 short conversations and 2 long conversations. At the end of each conversation, one or more questions will be asked about what was said. Both the conversation and the questions will be spoken only once. After each question there will be a pause. During the pause, you must read the four choices marked A), B), C) and D), and decide which is the best answer.)

1. A) College tuition has become a heavy burden for the students.

B) College students are in general politically active nowadays.

C) He took part in many protests when he was at college.

D) He is doubtful about the effect of the students' action,

2. A) The class has kept the party a secret from Jay.

B) Jay is organizing a party for the retiring dean.

C) Jay is surprised to learn of the party for him.

D) The dean will come to Jay's birthday party.

3. A) He found his wallet in his briefcase.

B) He went to the lost-and-found office.

C) He found the woman to go and pick up his car.

D) He left his things with his car in the garage.

4. A) The show he directed turned out lo be a success.

B) He watched only those comedies by famous directors.

C) TV comedies have not improved much since the 1960s.

D) New comedies are exciting, just like those in the 1960s.

5. A) The man should stop boiling the vegetables.

B) The man should try out some new recipes.

C) Overcooked vegetables are often tasteless.

D) All vegetables should be cooked fresh.

6. A) Help them tidy up the house.

B) Sort out their tax returns.

C) Help them to decode a message.

D) Figure out a way to avoid taxes.

7. A) The woman remains a total mystery to him.

B) The woman is still trying to finish her work.

C) He has devoted a whole month to his research.

D) He didn't expect to complete his work so soon.

8. A) He has failed to register for the course.

B) He would like to major in psychology too.

C) There should be more time for registration.

D) Developmental psychology is newly offered.

- **Long Conversation One**

Questions 9 to 11 are based on the conversation you have just heard.

9. A) The brilliant product design.

B) The unique craftsmanship.

C) The new color combinations.

D) The texture of the fabrics.

10. A) Fancy products.

B) Local handicrafts.

C) Traditional Thai silks.

D) Unique tourist attractions.

11. A) It will start tomorrow.

B) It will last only one day.

C) It will be out into the countryside.

D) It will be on the following weekend.

- **Long Conversation Two**

Questions 12 to 15 are based on the conversation you have just heard.

12. A) A year of practical training.

B) A happy childhood.

C) A pleasant neighborhood.

D) A good secondary education.

13. A) He is good at carpentry.

B) He is academically gifted.

C) He should be sent to a private school.

D) He ought to get good vocational training.

14. A) Donwell School.

B) Carlton Abbey.

C) Enderby High.

D) Enderby Comprehensive.

15. A) Find out more about the five schools.

B) Send their children to a better private school.

C) Talk with their children about their decision.

D) Put Keith in a good boarding school.

◇ Section B

Directions: In this section, you will hear three short passages. At the end of each passage, you will hear some questions. Both the passage and the questions will be spoken only once. After you hear a question, you must choose the best answer from the four choices marked A), B), C) and D).

- **Passage One**

Questions 16 to 18 are based on the passage you have just heard.

16. A) It will be ventilated.

B) It will be brightly lit.

C) It will provide easy access to the disabled.

D) It will have a large space for storage.

17. A) Opposite to the library.

B) On the same floor as the labs.

    C) On the first floor.

    D) On the ground floor.

18. A) To make the building appear traditional.

    B) To cut the construction cost to the minimum.

    C) To match the style of construction on the site.

    D) To embody the subcommittee's design concepts.

- **Passage Two**

Questions 19 to 22 are based on the passage you have just heard.

19. A) Sell financial software.

    B) Write financial software.

    C) Conduct research on financial software.

    D) Train clients to use financial software.

20. A) Rewarding.

    B) Unsuccessful.

    C) Tedious.

    D) Important.

21. A) He provided individual support.

    B) He held group discussions.

    C) He gave the trainees lecture notes.

    D) He offered online tutorial.

22. A) Nobody is able to solve all the problems in a couple of weeks.

    B) The fault might lie in his style of presenting the information.

    C) The trainees' problems has to be dealt with one by one.

    D) The employees were a bit slow to follow his instruction.

- **Passage Three**

Questions 23 to 25 are based on the passage you have just heard.

23. A) Their teachers meet them only in class.

    B) Their parents tend to overprotect them.

    C) They have little close contact with adults.

    D) They rarely read any books about adults.

24. A) Writers and lawyers are brought in to talk to students.

    B) Real-life cases are simulated for students to learn law.

    C) More Teacher and Writer Collaboratives are being set up.

    D) Opportunities are created for children to become writers.

25. A) Children like to form partnerships with each other.

    B) Children are often the best teachers of other children.

    C) Paired Learning cultivates the spirit of cooperation.

    D) Sixth-graders can teach first-graders as well as teachers.

◇ Section C

Directions: In this section, you will hear a passage three times. When the passage is read for the first time，you should listen carefully for its general idea. When the passage is read for the second time，you are required to fill in the blanks with the exact words you have just heard. Finally，when the passage is read for the third time，you should check what you have written.

Tests may be the most unpopular part of academic life. Students hate them because they produce fear and ___26___ about being evaluated, and focus on grades instead of learning for learning's sake.

But tests are also valuable. A well-constructed test ___27___ what you know and what you still need to learn. Tests help you see how your performance ___28___ to that of others. And knowing that you'll be tested on ___29___ material is certainly likely to ___30___ you to learn the material more thoroughly.

However, there's another reason you might dislike tests: You may assume that tests have the power to ___31___ your worth as a person. If you do badly on a test, you may be tempted to believe that you've received some ___32___ information about yourself from the professor, information that says you're a failure in some significant way.

This is a dangerous—and wrong-headed—assumption. If you do badly on a test, it doesn't mean you are a bad person or stupid. Or that you'll never do better again, and that your life is ___33___. If you don't do well on a test, you're the same person you were before you took the test — no better, no worse. You just did badly on a test.

That's it. ___34___, tests are not a measure of your value as an individual — they are a measure only of how well and how much you studied. Tests are tools; they are indirect and ___35___ measures of what we know.

Appendix A　Audio Scripts

■ Chapter 1

· **Compound Dictation One**

Leonardo's Speech

Thank you all so very much. Thank you to the Academy, thank you to all of you in this room. I have to congratulate the other incredible nominees this year for their unbelievable performances. The Revenant was the product of the tireless efforts of an unbelievable cast and crew I got to work alongside. First off, to my brother in this endeavor, Mr. Tom Hardy. Tom, your fierce talent on screen can only be surpassed by your friendship off screen. To Mr. Alejandro Innaritu, as the history of cinema unfolds, you have forged your way into history these past 2 years... thank you for creating a transcendent cinematic experience. Thank you to everybody at Fox and New Regency...my entire team. I have to thank everyone from the very onset of my career...to Mr. Jones for casting me in my first film to Mr. Scorsese for teaching me so much about the cinematic art form. To my parents, none of this would be possible without you. And to my friends, I love you dearly, you know who you are.

And lastly I just want to say this: making The Revenant was about man's relationship to the natural world. A world that we collectively felt in 2015 as the hottest year in recorded history. Our production needed to move to the southern tip of this planet just to be able to find snow. Climate change is real, it is happening right now. It is the most urgent threat facing our entire species, and we need to work collectively together and stop procrastinating.

We need to support leaders around the world who do not speak for the big polluters, but who speak for all of humanity, for the indigenous people of the world, for the billions and billions of underprivileged people out there who would be most affected by this. For our children's children, and for those people out there whose voices have been drowned out by the politics of greed. I thank you all for this amazing award tonight. Let us not take this planet for granted. I do not take tonight for granted. Thank you so very much.

· **Compound Dictation Two**

Jonathan Klein: Photos that changed the world

In my industry, we believe that images can change the world. Okay, we're naive, we're bright-eyed and bushy-tailed. The truth is that we know that the images themselves don't change the world, but we're also aware that, since the beginning of photography, images have provoked reactions in people, and those reactions have caused change to happen.

So let's begin with a group of images. I'd be extremely surprised if you didn't recognize many or most of them. They're best described as iconic, so iconic, perhaps they're cliches. In fact, they're so well-known that you might even recognize them in a slightly or somewhat different form. (Laughter)

But I think we're looking for something more. We're looking for something more. We're looking for images that shine an uncompromising light on crucial issues, images that transcend borders, that transcend religions, images that provoke us to step up and do something, in other words, to act. Well, this image, you've all seen. It changed our view of the physical world. We had never seen our planet from this perspective before. Many people credit a lot of the birth of the environmental movement to our seeing the planet like this for the first time, its smallness, its fragility 40 years later, this group, more than most, are well aware of the destructive power that our species can wield over our environment. And at last, we appear to be doing something about it. This destructive power takes many different forms. For example, these images taken by Brent Stirton in the Congo, these gorillas were murdered, some would even say crucified, and unsurprisingly, they sparked international outrage. Most recently, we've been tragically reminded of the destructive power of nature itself with the recent earthquake in Haiti.

What I think that is far worse is man's destructive power over man. Samuel Pisar, an Auschwitz survivor said, and I'll quote him, "The Holocaust teaches us that nature, even in its cruelest moments, is benign in comparison with man, when he loses his moral compass and his reason."

There's another kind of crucifixion. The horrifying images from Abu Ghraib as well as the images from Guantanamo had a profound impact. The publication of those images, as opposed to the images themselves, caused a government to change its policies. Some would argue that it is those images that did more to fuel the insurgency in Iraq than virtually any other single act. Furthermore, those images forever removed the so-called moral high ground of the occupying forces.

Let's go back a little. In the 1960s and 1970s, the Vietnam War was basically shown in America's living rooms day in, day out. News photos brought people face to face with the victims of the war, a little girl burned by napalm, a student killed by the National Guard at Kent State University in Ohio during a protest. In fact, these images became the voices of protest themselves. Now, images have power to shed light of understanding on suspicion, ignorance, and in particular—I've given a lot of talks on this but I'll just show one image—the issue of HIV/AIDS. In the 1980s the stigmatization of people with the disease was an enormous barrier to even discussing or addressing it. A simple act, in 1987, of the most famous woman in the world, the Princess of Wales, touching an HIV/AIDS infected baby, did a great deal, especially in Europe, to stop that. She, better than most, knew the power of an image.

So when we are confronted by a powerful image, we all have a choice. We can look away, or we can address the image. Thankfully, when these photos appeared in the Guardian in 1998, they put a lot of focus and attention, and in the end a lot of money, towards the Sudan famine relief efforts. Did the images change the world? No, but they had a major impact. Images often push us to question our core beliefs and our responsibilities to each other. We all saw those images after Katrina, and I think for millions of people, they had a very strong impact, and I think it's very unlikely that they were far from the minds of Americans when they went to vote in November 2008.

Unfortunately, some very important images are deemed too graphic or disturbing for us to see them. I'll show you one photo here, and it's a photo by Eugene Richards of an Iraq War veteran from an extraordinary piece of work, which has never been published, called "War is Personal." But images don't need to be graphic in order to remind us of the tragedy of war. John Moore set up this photo at Arlington cemetery. After all the tense moments of conflict, in all the conflict zones of the world, there's one photograph from a much quieter place that haunts me still, much more than the others.

Ansel Adams said, and I disagree with him, "You don't take a photograph, you make it." In my view, it's not the photographer who makes the photo, it's you. We bring to each image our own values, our own belief systems, and as a result of that, the image resonates with us. My company has 70 million images. I have one image in my office. Here it is. I hope that the next time you see an image that sparks something in you, you'll better understand why, and I know that, speaking to this audience, you'll definitely do something about it.

And thank you to all the photographers. (Applause)

◇ Section A

- **Conversation One**

M: Hi, Lisa.

W: Hi, Jeff. Hey, have you been to the art room today?

M: No, why?

W: Well, Mr. Jennings hung up a notice about a big project that's going on downtown. You know how the city's been doing a lot of work to fix up Main Street—you know, to make it look nicer? Well, they're going to create a mural.

M: You mean, like, make a painting on the entire wall of a building?

W: Exactly!

M: But where?

W: It's that big wall on the side of the public library. And students from this school are going to do the whole thing ... create a design, and paint it, and everything. I wish I could be a part of it, but I'm too busy.

M: Cool! I'd love to help design a mural. Imagine everyone in town walking past that wall and seeing my artwork, every day.

W: I thought you'd be interested. They want the mural to be about nature, so I guess all the design ideas students come up with should have a nature theme.

M: That makes sense—they've been planting so many trees and plants along the streets and in the park.

W: If you're interested you should talk with Mr. Jennings.

M: [half listening, daydreaming] This could be so much fun. Maybe I'll try to visit the zoo this weekend ... You know, to see the wild animals and get some ideas, something to inspire me!

W: Well maybe you should go to the art room first to get more information from Mr. Jennings.

M: Oh yeah. Good idea. Thanks for letting me know, Lisa! I'll go there right away.

Questions 1 to 4 are based on the conversation you have just heard.

1. What are the speakers mainly discussing?

2. Why is the boy excited?

3. Where does the boy say he may go this weekend?

4. Why does the girl suggest that the boy go to the art room?

- **Conversation Two**

M: Hi, Sarah. What's up?

W: Oh, hi, I just got out a history class. I had to give a presentation.

M: How did it go?

W: Terribly. I'm sure I made a fool of myself.

M: Why? Weren't you prepared?

W: No, it was not that. I just get so embarrassed and nervous whenever I have to speak in front of a group of people. I stand up and my face gets red and then I get even more nervous because I know everyone can see me blushing.

M: It's not so bad to blush.

W: But it happens all the time. If the professor asks a question and I know the answer, I blush like crazy if he calls on me. Doesn't that ever happen to you?

M: No, not really. Maybe you should just try to forget about the people. Look at something else in the room like the exit sign.

W: I guess I could try that but I doubt it'll help.

M: You know, we talked about it in psychology class. Blushing, even though it's involuntary, is more or less a learned behavior.

W: What do you mean?

M: Oh, children hardly ever blush at all. And among adults, supposedly, women blush more than men.

W: I wonder why?

M: I don't know, but I have a friend at high schools, Brian Smith. It was really easy to make him blush. He turned red whenever a waitress would ask him for his order.

W: I'm not that bad. Well, I've got to get going for my next class. I'll talk to you later.

Questions 5 to 8 are based on the conversation you have just heard.

5. What was the woman's problem?
6. Why might looking at the exit sign help the woman?
7. What does the man say about children?
8. Why does the man mention his friend Brian Smith?

◇ Section B

· Passage One

In the case of mobile phones, change is everything. Recent research indicates that the mobile phone is changing not only our culture, but our very bodies as well.

First, let's talk about culture. The difference between the mobile phone and its parent, the fixed-line phone, you get whoever answers it.

This has several implications. The most common one, however, and perhaps the thing that has changed our culture forever, is the "meeting" influence. People no longer need to make firm plans about when and where to meet. Twenty years ago, a Friday night would need to be arranged in advance. You needed enough time to allow everyone to get from their place of work to the first meeting place. Now, however, a night out can be arranged on the run. It is no longer "see you there at 8", but "text me around 8 and we'll see where we all are". Texting changes people as well. In their paper, "insights into the Social and Psychological Effects of SMS Text Messaging", two British researchers distinguished between two types of mobile phone users: the "talkers" and the "texters"—those who prefer voice to text message and those who prefer text to voice. They found that the mobile phone's individuality and privacy gave texters the ability to express a whole new outer personality. Texters were likely to report that their family would be surprised if they were to read their texts. This suggests that texting allowed texters to present a self-image that differed from the one familiar to those who knew them well.

Another scientist wrote of the changes that mobiles have brought to body language. There are two kinds that people use while speaking on the phone. There is the "speakeasy": the head is held high, in a self-confident way, chatting away. And there is the "spacemaker": these people focus on themselves and keep out other people.

Who can blame them? Phone meetings get cancelled or reformed and camera—phones intrude on people's privacy. So, it is understandable if your mobile makes you nervous. But perhaps you needn't worry so much. After all, it is good to talk.

Questions 9 to 11 are based on the passage you have just heard.

9. What does recent research indicate about the mobile phone?

10. What may people do when they plan to meet nowadays?

11. What do we learn from the passage about the texts sent by texters?

- **Passage Two**

Music which is original is individual and personal. That is to say, it can be identified as belonging to a particular composer. It has particular qualities, or a style, which are not copied from another. If you can recognize the style of a composer, you will probably be able to tell that a certain composition belongs to him or her even though you have never heard it before. A basket-maker has the skill of weaving his materials to create colorful patterns, and an expert carpenter has the skill of joining together different shapes and sizes of wood to make a beautiful piece of furniture. These skills may be referred to as "workmanship". Similarly, in music a composer organizes his melodies and rhythms and combines sounds to create harmony. A composer may be capable of thinking up very good and original tunes, yet if tunes are poorly organized the final result will not be standard. Good music expresses feelings in a way that is suitable to those feelings. There may be joy, sorrow, fear, love, anger, or whatever. Bad music, on the other hand, may confuse unrelated feelings, it may not express any important feelings at all, or it may exaggerate some feelings and make them vulgar.

Good music will stand the test of time. It will gain a kind of permanent status while bad music will disappear and be forgotten quickly. In pop music, where the general rule seems to be "the newer the better", the test of time is the hardest test of all to pass.

Questions 12 to 15 are based on the passage you have just heard

12. What is the feature of a piece of original music?

13. How are feelings expressed in a piece of good music?

14. What does the passage say about the relationship between time and music?

15. What do we learn about pop music according to the passage?

◈ Section C

- **Recording One**

A few years ago, in their search for ways to sell more goods, advertising men hit on a new and controversial trick. It's a silent, invisible commercial that, the admen claim, can be rushed past the consumer's conscious mind and planted in his subconscious and without the consumer's knowledge.

Developed by James Vicary, a research man who studies what makes people buy, this technique relies on the psychological principle of subconscious perception. Scientists tell us that many of the sights coming to our eyes are not consciously "seen." We select only a few for conscious "seeing," and ignore the rest—at least we think we do. Actually these discarded impressions are recorded in the brain. The "discarded" impressions are examples of subconscious perception: that is, they are below the threshold of consciousness.

There's little doubt in Vicary's mind as to the subconscious ad's effectiveness. His proof can be summed up in just two words: sales increases. In an unidentified New Jersey movie house not so long ago, unknowing audiences saw a curious film program. At the same time, on the same screen on which the film hero was courting the heroine, or the detective was trailing his suspect, a subconscious projector was flashing its invisible commercials."Get popcorn," ordered the commercial for a reported one three-thousandths of a second every five seconds. It announced "Coca Cola" at the same speed and frequency to other audiences. At the end of a six weeks trial, popcorn sales had gone up 57 per cent, Coke sales 18 per cent.

A New Orleans firm, Experimental Films, Inc, says the technique is not new. It began research on subconscious perception in 1954 at Loyola University. Experimental Films stresses that its equipment was designed for use in helping problem students and treating the mentally ill. At NYU two doctors with the Research Center for Mental Health showed twenty women the projected image of an expressionless face. They told the subjects to watch the face for some change of expression. Then they flashed the word angry on the screen at subconscious speeds. Now the women thought the face looked unpleasant. When the word happy was flashed on the screen instead, the subjects thought that the woman's facial expression looked much more pleasant.

Subconscious techniques, its promoters believe, are good for more than selling popcorn. Perhaps the process can even be used to sell political candidates. Just leave a favorable impression of the candidate in the minds of the electorate—subconsciously, of course.

Just how convincing are these invisible commercials? Skeptical psychologists answer that they aren't anywhere near as effective as the admen would like to think. Nothing has been proved yet scientifically, says a prominent research man.

Questions 16 to 19 are based on the recording you have just heard.

16. What is subconscious perception according to the speaker?

17. To advertising sponsors, what is the true test of subconscious projection?

18. What are some psychologists' attitudes toward subconscious projection?

19. What is the author's position on subconscious projection in ads?

· **Recording Two**

Hi, I am Paddy Kim. I would like to elaborate what a severe situation we are facing in terms of water shortage. A new study warns that about thirty percent of the world's people will not have enough water by the year 2025. The report says lack of water in the future may result in several problems. It may increase health problems. Lack of water often means drinking water is not safe. There are problems all over the world because of disease such as cholera that is carried in water. Lack of water also may result in more international conflict. Countries may have to fight for water in the future. Some countries now get sixty percent of their fresh water from other countries. This is true of Egypt, the Netherlands, Cambodia, Syria, Sudan and Iraq. And the report says lack of water would affect the ability to improve their economies. This is because new industries often need a large amount of water when they are beginning.

Therefore, it is necessary and urgent for us to launch water saving campaign. We could begin it from our daily activities.Whether you're getting ready to take a bath in the morning, or just soaking in the shower at the end of a long day, the bathroom can be a retreat from the world, but it's also where over 60 percent of the water used indoors gets consumed. So if you'd like to save water and money, the bathroom is a great place to start. Let's take a look at the biggest consumer of water in the bathroom, the toilet. Toilets made before 1993 use up to 8 gallons of water per flush, compared to only 1.6 gallons used by modern fixtures. It's a good idea to replace pre-1993 toilets if you can. Now if you are not sure exactly how old your toilet is, well, all you have to do is take the lid off the tank and check out the underside because usually there is a manufacturing date stamped underneath. Even if you can't replace your toilet right away, you can still save water using a one-liter plastic bottle. Just fill the bottle with some pebbles or sand, put the cap back on and place it in your tank. So it reduces the water used with each flush.

Believe it or not, plumbing leaks account for about 14 percent of the water used in the average home, so it's a good idea to check your toilet for leaks. Here is how. Put five to ten drops of food coloring into the tank. Now put the lid back on, but don't flush, wait about 15 minutes, and check the toilet bowl. If you see any food coloring, there is a leak that's wasting water. With a few simple changes right here in the bathroom, you can keep plenty of water and money from going straight down the drain.

Questions 20 to 22 are based on the recording you have just heard.

20. What does lack of water usually mean according to the new study?

21. What is the speaker's advice to start with to save water?

22. What can the food coloring be used to do?

• Recording Three

The White House was the largest house in the country until after the Civil War in the 1860s. The White House has 132 rooms, including 16 family and guest rooms, 35 bathrooms and three kitchens. There are six levels. The first level has many famous rooms. For example, the West Wing of the White House includes the Oval Office. This is where the president works and meets with his advisers. The president receives guests in the Blue Room. And the State Dining Room can hold 140 people for official dinners in honor of foreign leaders.

The second and third floors are the family's private areas. When it is cold outside, the president and his family can warm up near one of the White House's 28 fireplaces. And when it is hot outside, they can swim in the outdoor pool.

The White House offers lot of things to do for entertainment. The first family can watch a movie in the small theater, play ping-pong in the family game room or bowl in the small bowling alley. Former President Richard Nixon had the bowling alley built in nineteen sixty-nine. The White House's newest occupant, Barack Obama, is not much of a bowler. But he is a big fan of basketball. He has already been seen shooting hoops on the basketball court outside. President Obama is said to be considering replacing the bowling alley with an indoor basketball court.

The Obama family recently added an outdoor playground for their two young daughters. It has a swing set, a climbing section, a slide and a tire for swinging. The Obamas can also play tennis on a court on the South Lawn, hit a few golf balls on the putting greens or run around the jogging track.

The White House has been home to forty-three presidents. America's first president, George Washington supervised the building process which began in 1792. But he never lived there. John and Abigail Adams became the building's first family in 1800. Since then, the White House has experienced many changes. And each presidential family has left its own historical mark on America's most famous house.

Questions 23 to 25 are based on the recording you have just heard.

23. Where does the president usually receive his guests?

24. What did President Nixon do for entertainment in 1969, according to the speaker?

25. Who was the first president that lived in the White House?

■ Chapter 2

• Compound Dictation One

Hardest Languages

How difficult a language is to learn is often a matter of perspective. For example, a Dutch speaker trying to learn German will have a much easier time than, say, a Mandarin speaker because Dutch and German are closely related languages and Mandarin and German are not, so get ready to find out about the 5 most difficult languages in the world to learn. Hungarian stands as several odd men out in Europe alongside Finnish and Estonian as belonging to a language family other than that of a majority of European languages. Most European languages belong to a family called Indo-European but Hungarian belongs to a family called Finno-Ugric. What makes Hungarian incredibly difficult to learn for say German or English speaker is the combination of incredibly alien vocabulary combined with insanely difficult grammar. For example, German and English have many words in common with each other, such as finger and Finger (德语), beer and bier (德语) and wolf and Wolf (德语). But if you line up those same words with Hungarian you can see where the difficulty comes in, finger and uii (匈牙利语), beer and sor (匈牙利语) and wolf and farkas (匈牙利语). They are completely different, making it a true challenge to learn. There really is no such thing as Chinese. Rather what is normally called Chinese or Chinese dialects are in fact different languages. Mandarin is the official language of China, but there are others, most prominently the Cantonese language which is spoken in southern China as well as in Hong Kong and Macao. Mandarin has four different tones, each of which conveys a different meaning and can be difficult enough to get right for a foreigner but Cantonese has six tones. Additionally the real difficulty in learning Chinese is always the reading and writing system because the language has no alphabet. Instead it uses an archaic writing system based on one called ideograms. Ideograms are graphic symbols that convey meaning and the Chinese ones were originally based on representation of things from the real world. Over time the relationship between the symbols and what they represented was lost, but the complexity in the number of characters grew. It takes years and years even as a Chinese person to learn enough of the characters to be literate. Compare that to Korean alphabet Hangul which can be learned in a few hours and you get an idea of how difficult it can be to acquire even basic literacy. Given this the Chinese writing system was reformed in the twentieth century in mainland China into what is called simplified characters but in HK they kept the even more complex traditional ones which, when combined with a greater number of tones, makes HK Cantonese one of the most difficult languages in the world to learn. Xhosa is a language that belongs to the African family of languages called Bantu and it is one of the official languages of south Africa. In addition to a difficult grammar and vocabulary foreign to native speakers of English, it is one of the intimate clicking sound of language that requires unique precision in order to pronounce correctly. The language has totaled 18 clicks that are very hard for non-natives to learn. So if you decide to pick up Xhosa, all we can say is Good Luck. You are going to need it. Navajo is an American Indian language and it has an unusual role in history due to its isolation as a language and small number of speakers. During WWII a man named Philip Johnston suggested the introduction of so-called Navajo code talkers in order to preserve the secrecy of information and confuse the enemy. He was fortunate to grow up as a son of missionary in a reservation and thus spoke it fluently. But he also realized that almost no one spoke it and those who tried usually failed. Considering its distinguishing tense which refers to when something happened as we do in English, Navajo instead uses something called ASPECT which stresses the way something was done instead of when it was done. These have no real correspondence in English but of classifications such as transitional which involves action involving transition from one status of a form to another momentaneous which involves the action that takes place at a specific point of time and many others. You can see why Nava beheld and learned and why the Novojo code talkers were able to outwit the Japanese at every turn. If you thought Navajo will be hard to learn, then Greenlandic is just off the charts. It's one of the Eskimo languages spoken by the Inuit of Greenland and its incredibly strange and difficult grammar makes it the most difficult language to learn. Besides being unrelated to anything western or eastern people are familiar with, it is the grammar that is the real killer. Most languages have distinctive parts for subjects, objects and verbs, but in Greenlandic a verb itself contains virtually all information of the things conveyed in the sentence including the subject and object, making the language conceptually very different from anything you might have encountered in a language learning classroom.

- ### **Compound Dictation Two**

Don't Insist on English

I know what you're thinking. You think I've lost my way. Somebody's going to come on the stage in a minute and guide me gently back to my seat. (Applause) I get that all the time in Dubai. "Here on the holiday are you, dear?" (Laughter) "Come to visit the children? How long are you staying?" Well actually, I hope for a while longer yet. I have been living and teaching in the Gulf for over 30 years. (Applause) And in that time, I have seen a lot of changes. Now that statistic is quite shocking. And I want to talk to you today about language loss and the globalization of English. I want to tell you about my friend who was teaching English to adults in Abu Dhabi. And one fine day, she decided to take them into the garden to teach them some nature vocabulary. But it was she who ended up learning all the Arabic words for the local plants, as well as their uses, medicinal uses, cosmetics (化妆用的), cooking, herbal(草本的). How did those students get all that knowledge? Of course, from their grandparents and even their great-grandparents. It's not necessary to tell you how important it is to be able to communicate across generations. But sadly, today, languages are dying at an unprecedented(前所未有的) rate. A language dies every 14 days. Now, at the same time, English is the undisputed (不可置疑的) global language. Could there be a connection? Well I don't know. But I do know that I've seen a lot of changes. When I first came out to the Gulf, I came to Kuwait in the days when it was still a hardship post. Actually, not that long ago. That is a little bit too early. But nevertheless, I was recruited by the British Council, along with about 25 other teachers. And we were the first non-Muslims to teach in the state schools there in Kuwait. We were brought to teach English because the government wanted to modernize the country and to empower (授权，使能够) the citizens through education. And of course, the U.K. benefited from some of that lovely oil wealth.

Okay. Now this is the major change that I've seen—how teaching English has morphed (变体) from being a mutually beneficial practice to becoming a massive (大规模的) international business that it is today. No longer just a foreign language on the school curriculum (课程), and no longer the sole domain (唯一的领域) of mother England, it has become a bandwagon for every English-speaking nation on earth. And why not? After all, the best education — according to the latest World University Rankings (等级，排名)—is to be found in the universities of the U.K. and the U.S. So everybody wants to have an English education naturally. But if you're not a native speaker, you have to pass a test. Now can it be right to reject a student on linguistic ability alone? Perhaps you have a computer scientist who's a genius. Would he need the same language as a lawyer, for example? Well, I don't think so. We English teachers reject them all the time. We put a stop sign and we stop them in their tracks. They can't pursue their dream any longer till they get English. Now let me put it this way: if I met a monolingual Dutch speaker who had the cure for cancer, would I stop him from entering my British University? I don't think so. But indeed, that is exactly what we do. We English teachers are the gatekeepers (看门人). And you have to satisfy us first that your English is good enough. Now it can be dangerous to give too much power to a narrow segment (狭隘的部分) of society. Maybe the barrier would be too universal.

Okay. "But," I hear you say, "what about the research? It's all in English." So the books are in English, the journals are done in English, but that is a self-fulfilling (自我实现的) prophecy (预言能力). It feeds the English requirement. And so it goes on. I ask you, what happened to translation? If you think about the Islamic Golden Age, there was lots of translation then. They translated from Latin and Greek into Arabic, into Persian, and then it was translated on into the Germanic languages of Europe and the Romance languages. And so light shone upon the Dark Ages of Europe.

Now don't get me wrong; I am not against teaching English, all you English teachers out there. I love it that we have a global language. We need one today more than ever. But I am against using it as a barrier. Do we really want to end up with 600 languages and the main one being English, or Chinese? We need more than that. Where do we draw the line? This system equates (相当于) intelligence with a knowledge of English, which is quite arbitrary. (Applause) And I want to remind you that the giants upon whose shoulders today's intelligents stand did not have to pass an English test. Case in point, Einstein. He, by the way, was considered remedial at school because he was, in fact, dyslexic (读写困难). But fortunately for the world, he did not have to pass an English test. Because they didn't start until 1964 with TOEFL, the American test of English. Now it's exploded. There are lots and lots of tests of English. And millions and millions of students take these tests every year. Now you might think, you and me, "Those fees aren't bad, they're okay," but they are prohibitive (禁止的) to so many millions of poor people. So immediately, we're rejecting them. (Applause)

It brings to mind a headline I saw recently: "Education: The Great Divide." Now I get it, I understand why people would want to focus on English. They want to give their children the best chance in life. And to do that, they need a Western education. Because, of course, the best jobs go to people out of the Western Universities, that I put on earlier. It's a circular thing.

Okay. Let me tell you a story about two scientists, two English scientists. They were doing an experiment to do with genetics and the forelimbs and the hind limbs (前肢和后肢) of animals. But they couldn't get the results they wanted. They really didn't know what to do, until along came a German scientist who realized that they were using two words for forelimb and hind limb, whereas genetics does not differentiate and neither does German. So bingo, problem solved. If you can't think a thought, you are stuck. But if another language can think that thought, then, by cooperating, we can achieve and learn so much more.

My daughter came to England from Kuwait. She had studied science and mathematics in Arabic. It's an Arabic medium school. She had to translate it into English at her grammar school. And she was the best in the class at those subjects. Which tells us that when students come to us from abroad, we may not be giving them enough credit (荣誉，信任)for what they know, and they know it in their own language. When a language dies, we don't know what we lose with that language.

This is—I don't know if you saw it on CNN recently—they gave the Heroes Award to a young Kenyan shepherd (牧羊的) boy who couldn't study at night in his village, like all the village children, because the kerosene lamp (煤油灯). It had smoke and it damaged his eyes. And anyway, there was never enough kerosene, because what does a dollar a day buy for you? So he invented a cost-free solar lamp. And now the children in his village get the same grades at school as the children who have electricity at home. And when…(Applause) When he received his award, he said these lovely words: "The children can lead Africa from what it is today, a dark continent, to a light continent." A simple idea, but it could have such far-reaching consequences. People who have no light, whether it's physical or metaphorical, cannot pass our exams, and we can never know what they know. Let us not keep them and ourselves in the dark. Let us celebrate diversity. Mind your language. Use it to spread great ideas.(Applause)

Thank you very much.

• *Video Appreciation : My Big Fat Greek Wedding*

So, it was just me, all alone... up in the mountains in this cottage, all summer.

Don't all your cousins go up, too?

No. I only have two cousins. They live in Wisconsin.

You only have two cousins?

Yeah. How many do you have?

More than two.

Well, who else? Don't you have brothers or sisters? What are your parents like?

What?

Well....

Okay, Christmas. What do you do for Christmas

My mum makes roast lamb.

With mint jelly?

No.

And?

And...I'm Greek, right? So what happens is, my dad and my uncles fight over who gets to eat the lamb brain. And then my Aunt Voula forked the eyeball land chases me around... trying to make me eat it, because it'll make me smart. You have two cousins. I have 27 first cousins. Just 27 first cousins alone. And my whole family is big and loud... and everybody's in each other's lives and business all the time. You never have a minute alone to think, because we're always together eating, eating and eating. The only people we know are Greeks, because Greeks marry Greeks, to breed more Greeks... to be loud, breeding Greek eater.

Wow!

I'm serious. No one in my family has ever gone out with a non Greek before. No one. And you're … you're just, you know, wonderful. But I just don't see how this is going to work out. So...

Work out? What's to work out? We're not a different species. Yes, we come from different back grounds... and, hey, here's some news about my life, to this point. It's boring. Then I met you and you're interesting and you're beautiful and fun. You've got a weird family. Who doesn't? I just feel like we can't get married, not like this. It's like... when I'm with you.. I am so happy... But my family is so unhappy. And our wedding should be this joyous thing. But it won't be for them because it can't be in our church. So let's just go somewhere. Please, let's just go...

Hey, I love you.

Why? Why do you love me?

Because I came alive when I met you.

But my family...

You are a part of your family, and I'll do anything... Whatever it takes to let them accept me. Because you're my whole life now. We're not going to skulk off and get married...as if we are ashamed of ourselves. Okay?

Did you say skulk?

Shut up.

Let's just skulk off somewhere.

Come on, talk to him. Toula loves him. Do it for Toula, come on. Come on. He wants to get married in the church. Go!

All right. So, you're going to be baptized tomorrow?

Yeah.

It's your lucky day to be baptized in the Greek Orthodox Church. Nicky is gonna be your godmother. You know, the word "baptism"...comes from the Greek word "baftisia." That's where we dip the baby in a beautiful, little silver basin.

It's not so bad.

Are you kidding? Any minute now, he's going to look at me and go: Right. You're so not worth this.

Yes, you are.

I'm Greek now.

Thank you so much.

(meeting Toula's family)

So, for "Happy Easter," we say "Kbristos Anesti." Then the other person says back, "Alitbos Anesti." So if you want to say "Happy Easter," you go, "Kbristos Anesti." You try.

"Kbristos Anesti."

That's good.

Hey, Dad.

Mr. Portokalos, Kbristos Anesti. (Greek)

He likes you!

I've told you to watch the boys.

They'll be fine with the video games.

You turn their brains to mush. I can't do anything right. Ian, if you're going to be in this family, I'll get you some earplugs... because the Portokalos women, if they're not nagging somebody, they die!

You're in trouble when I tell my sister.

Tell me what?

Where is he?

Kbristos Anesti.

Toula Toula, you're engaged. We never think it would happen for you. Never. Taki,didn't we say that?

We never think this day will come. And it came!

Is it him?

Yes, sorry. Everyone, this is Ian.

Ian!

(meeting Ian's parents)

Silence!

En?

Delicious.

We took a look at my calendar, our calender... to set a day for the big day...sometime at the end of October...mid November? Sometime in there, yeah.

Wonderful. I'll call that club to see what's open.

The club?

The North Shore Country Club. For the wedding of course.

We're going to get married in Toula's church because we are not very religious and her family is. Really is. Show them the brochure.

My cousin Nicky made me this. She tends to save things. This is from her prom. She makes lamps and…

Tell them about… we got this great big hall. What's it called for the reception?

Aphrodite's Palace. It's not really a palace. This is the brochure. That Parthenon backdrop is optional.

◇ Section A

- **Conversation One**

W: So Mike, you managed the innovation project at CucinTech.

M: I did indeed.

W: Well then, first, congratulations! It seems to have been very successful.

M: Thanks, yes. I really helped things turn around at CucinTech.

W: Was the revival in their fortunes entirely due to strategic innovation?

M: Yes, yes I think it was. CucinTech was a company who were very much following the pack, doing what everyone else was doing, and getting rapidly left behind. I could see there was a lot of talent there, and some great potential—particularly in their product development. I just have to harness that somehow.

W: Was innovation at the core of the project?

M: Absolutely. If it doesn't sound like too much of a cliché, our world is constantly changing, and it's changing quickly. We need to be innovating constantly to keep up with this. Stand still, and you're lost.

W: No stopping to sniff the roses?

M: Well, I'll do that in my personal life, sure. But as a business strategy, I'm afraid there's no stopping.

W: What exactly is strategic innovation then?

M: Strategic innovation is the process of managing innovation, of making sure it takes place at all levels of the company, and that it's related to the company's overall strategy.

W: I see.

M: So, instead of innovation for innovation's sake and new products being created simply because the technology is there, the company culture must switch from these point-in-time innovations to a continuous pipeline of innovations from everywhere and everyone.

W: How did you align strategies throughout the company?

M: I soon became aware that campaigning is useless. People take no notice. Simply it came about through good practice trickling down. This built consent—people could see it was the best way to work.

W: Does innovation on this scale really give a competitive advantage?

M: I am certain of it. Absolutely. Especially if it's difficult for a competitor to copy. The risk is, of course, that innovation may frequently lead to imitation.

W: But not if ifs strategic?

M: Precisely!

W: Thanks for talking to us.

M: Sure.

Questions 1 to 4 are based on the conversation you have just heard.

1. What seems to have been very successful according to the woman speaker?
2. What did the company lack before the man's scheme was implemented?
3. What does the man say he should do in his business?
4. What does the man say is the risk of innovation?

- **Conversation Two**

M: Today my guest is Dana Ivanovich who has worked for the last twenty years as an interpreter. Dana, welcome.

W: Thank you.

M: Now I'd like to begin by saying that I have on occasions used an interpreter myself, as a foreign correspondent, so I am full of admiration for what you do. But I think your profession is sometimes underrated, and many people think anyone who speaks more than one language can do it...

W: There aren't any interpreters I know who don't have professional qualifications and training. You only really get proficient after many years in the job.

M: And am I right in saying you can divide what you do into two distinct methods, simultaneous and consecutive interpreting?

W: That's right. The techniques you use are different, and a lot of interpreters will say one is easier than the other, less stressful.

M: Simultaneous interpreting, putting someone's words into another language more or less as they speak, sounds to me like the more difficult.

W: Well, actually no, most people in the business would agree that consecutive interpreting is the more stressful. You have to wait for the speaker to deliver quite a chunk of language, before you then put it into the second language, which puts your short term memory under intense stress.

M: You make notes, I presume.

W: Absolutely, anything like numbers, names, places, have to be noted down, but the rest is never translated word for word. You have to find a way of summarising it so that the message is there. Turning every single word into the target language would put too much strain on the interpreters and slow down the whole process too much.

M: But with simultaneous interpreting, you start translating almost as soon as the other person starts speaking. You must have some preparation beforehand.

W: Well, hopefully the speakers will let you have an outline of the topic a day or two in advance. You have a little time to do research, prepare technical expressions and so on.

Questions 5 to 8 are based on the conversation you have just heard.

5. What are the speakers mainly talking about?

6. What does the man think of Dana's profession?

7. What does Dana say about the interpreters she knows?

8. What do most interpreters think of consecutive interpreting?

◇ Section B

• **Passage One**

Mothers have been warned for years that sleeping with their newborn infant is a bad idea because it increases the risk that the baby might die unexpectedly during the night. But now Israeli researchers are reporting that even sleeping in the same room can have negative consequences, not for the child, but for the mother. Mothers who slept in the same room as their infants, whether in the same bed or just the same room, had poorer sleep than mothers whose babies slept elsewhere in the house: They woke up more frequently, were awake approximately 20 minutes longer per night, and had shorter periods of uninterrupted sleep. These results held true even taking into account that many of the women in the study were breast-feeding their babies. Infants, on the other hand, didn't appear to have worse sleep whether they slept in the same or different room from their mothers. The researchers acknowledge that since the families they studied were all middle-class Israelis, it's possible the results would be different in different cultures. Lead author Liat Tikotzky wrote in an email that the research team also didn't measure fathers' sleep, so it's possible that their sleep patterns could also be causing the sleep disruptions for moms. Right now, to reduce the risk of sudden infant death syndrome, the American Academy of Pediatrics recommends that mothers not sleep in the same beds as their babies, but sleep in the same room. The Israeli study suggests that doing so may be best for baby, but may take a toll on Mom.

Questions 9 to 11 are based on the passage you have just heard.

9.   What is the long-held view about mothers sleeping with newborn babies?

10.   What do Israeli researchers' findings show?

11.   What does the American Academy of Pediatrics recommend mothers do?

•   **Passage Two**

The US has already lost more than a third of the native languages that existed before European colonization and the remaining 192 are classed by the UNESCO as ranging between unsafe and extinct. "We need more funding and more effort to return these languages to everyday use," says Fred Nahwooksy of the National museum of the American Indian, "we are making progress, but money needs to be spent on revitalizing languages, not just documenting them." Some 40 languages mainly in California and Oklahoma where thousands of Indians were forced to relocate in the 19th century have fewer than 10 native speakers. Part of the issue is that tribal groups themselves don't always believe their languages are endangered until they are down to the last handful of speakers.

"But progress is being made through immersion schools, because if you teach children when they are young, it will stay with them as adults and that's the future." says Mr Nahwooksy, a Comanche Indian. Such schools have become a model in Hawaii, but the islanders' local language is still classed by the UNESCO as critically endangered because only 1,000 people speak it. The decline in the American Indian languages has historical roots: In the mid-19th century, the US government adopted a policy of Americanizing Indian children by removing them from their homes and culture. Within a few generations most had forgotten their native tongues. Another challenge to language survival is television. It has brought English into homes, and pushed out traditional storytelling and family time together, accelerating the extinction of native languages.

Questions 12 to 15 are based on the passage you have just heard.

12. What do we learn from the report?

13. For what purpose does Fred Nahwooksy appeal for more funding?

14. What is the historical cause of the decline in the American Indian Languages?

15. What does the speaker say about television?

◇ Section C

· Recording One

W: Grag Rosen lost his job as a sales manager nearly three years ago, and is still unemployed.

M: It literally is like something in a dream to remember what is like to actually be able to go out and put in a day's work and receive a day's pay.

W: At first, Rosen bought groceries and made house payments with the help from unemployment insurance. It pays laid-off workers up to half of their previous wages while they look for work. But now that insurance has run out for him and he has to make tough choices. He's cut back on medications and he no longer helps support his disabled mother. It is devastating experience. New research says the US recession is now over. But many people remain unemployed and unemployed workers face difficult odds. There is literally only one job opening for every five unemployed workers. So four out of five unemployed workers have actually no chance of finding a new job. Businesses have downsized or shut down across America, leaving fewer job opportunities for those in search of work. Experts who monitor unemployment statistics here in Bucks County, Pennsylvania, say about 28,000 people are unemployed, and many of them are jobless due to no fault of their own. That's where the Bucks County CareerLink comes in. Local director Elizabeth Walsh says they provide training and guidance to help unemployed workers find local job opportunities. "So here's the job opening, here's the job seeker, match them together under one roof," she said. But the lack of work opportunities in Bucks County limits how much she can help. Rosen says he hopes Congress will take action. This month he launched the 99ers Union, an umbrella organization of 18 Internet-based grassroots groups of 99ers. Their goal is to convince lawmakers to extend unemployment benefits. But Pennsylvania State Representative Scott Petri says governments simply do not have enough money to extend unemployment insurance. He thinks the best way to help the long-term unemployed is to allow private citizens to invest in local companies that can create more jobs. But the boost in investor confidence needed for the plan to work will take time. Time that Rosen says still requires him to buy food and make monthly mortgage payments. Rosen says he'll use the last of his savings to try to hang onto the home he worked for more than 20 years to buy. But once that money is gone, he says he doesn't know what he'll do.

Questions 16 to 18 are based on the recording you have just heard.

16. How does unemployment insurance help the unemployed?

17. What is local director Elizabeth Walsh of the Bucks County CareerLink doing?

18. What does Pennsylvania State Representative Scott Petri say is the best way to help the long-term unemployed?

- **Recording Two**

W: Earlier this year, British explorer Pen Huddle and his team trekked for three months across the frozen Arctic Ocean, taking measurements and recording observations about the ice.

M: Well we'd been led to believe that we would encounter a good proportion of this older, thicker, technically multi-year ice that's been around for a few years and just gets thicker and thicker. We actually found there wasn't any multi-year ice at all.

W: Satellite observations and submarine surveys over the past few years had shown less ice in the polar region, but the recent measurements show the loss is more pronounced than previously thought.

M: We're looking at roughly 80 percent loss of ice cover on the Arctic Ocean in 10 years, roughly 10 years, and 100 percent loss in nearly 20 years.

W: Cambridge scientist Peter Wadhams, who's been measuring and monitoring the Arctic since 1971 says the decline is irreversible.

M: The more you lose, the more open water is created, the more warming goes on in that open water during the summer, the less ice forms in winter, the more melt there is the following summer. It becomes a breakdown process where everything ends up accelerating until it's all gone.

W: Martin Sommerkorn runs the Arctic program for the environmental charity the World Wildlife Fund.

M: The Arctic sea ice holds a central position in the Earth's climate system and it's deteriorating faster than expected. Actually it has to translate into more urgency to deal with the climate change problem and reduce emissions.

W: Summerkorn says a plan to reduce greenhouse gas emissions blamed for global warming needs to come out of the Copenhagen Climate Change Summit in December.

M: We have to basically achieve there the commitment to deal with the problem now. That's the minimum. We have to do that equitably and we have to find a commitment that is quick.

W: Wadhams echoes the need for urgency.

M: The carbon that we've put into the atmosphere keeps having a warming effect for 100 years. So we have to cut back rapidly now, because it will take a long time to work its way through into a response by the atmosphere. We can't switch off global warming just by being good in the future, we have to start being good now.

W: Wadhams says there is no easy technological fix to climate change. He and other scientists say there are basically two options to replacing fossil fuels, generating energy with renewables, or embracing nuclear power.

Questions 19 to 22 are based on the recording you have just heard.

19. What did Pen Huddle and his team do in the Arctic Ocean?

20. What does the report say about the Arctic region?

21. What does Cambridge scientist Peter Wadhams say in his study?

22. How does Peter Wadhams view climate change?

· **Recording Three**

M: From a very early age, some children exhibit better self-control than others. Now, a new study that began with about 1,000 children in New Zealand has tracked how a child's low self-control can predict poor health，money troubles and even a criminal record in their adult years. Researchers have been studying this group of children for decades now. Some of their earliest observations have to do with the level of self-control the youngsters displayed. Parents, teachers, even the kids themselves, scored the youngsters on measures like "acting before thinking" and "persistence in reaching goals." The children of the study are now adults in their 30s. Terrie Moffitt of Duke University and her research colleagues found that kids with self-control issues tended to grow up to become adults with a far more troubling set of issues to deal with.

W: The children who had the lowest self-control when they were aged 3 to 10, later on had the most health problems in their 30s, and they had the worst financial situation. And they were more likely to have a criminal record and to be raising a child as a single parent on a very low income.

M: Speaking from New Zealand via skype, Moffitt explained that self-control problems were widely observed, and weren't just a feature of a small group of misbehaving kids.

W: Even the children who had above-average self-control as pre-schoolers, could have benefited from more self-control training. They could have improved their financial situation and their physical and mental health situation 30 years later.

M: So, children with minor self-control problems were likely as adults to have minor health problems, and so on. Moffitt said it's still unclear why some children have better self-control than others, though she says other researchers have found that it's mostly a learned behavior, with relatively little genetic influence. But good self-control can be set to run in families in that children who have good self-control are more likely to grow up to be healthy and prosperous parents.

W: Whereas some of the low-self-control study members are more likely to be single parents with a very low income and the parent is in poor health and likely to be a heavy substance abuser. So that's not a good atmosphere for a child. So it looks as though self-control is something that in one generation can disadvantage the next generation.

M: But the good news is that Moffitt says self-control can be taught by parents and through school curricula that have proved to be effective. Terrie Moffitt's paper on the link between childhood self-control and adult status decades later is published in the Proceedings of the National Academy of Sciences.

Questions 23 to 25 are based on the recording you have just heard.

23. What is the new study about?

24. What does the study seem to show?

25. What does Moffitt say is the good news from their study?

■ Chapter 3

• **Compound Dictation One**

Russia vs American German vs Greek

In August 2015, Russia reportedly destroyed 300 tons of food from nations which had imposed sanctions on them. These actions have served as an affront to western countries like the United States which has spent much of the last century locked in battles with the Soviets. A 2015 poll found that more than 80% of Russians have negative opinions about the United States compared to 34% in 2012. So why does Russia hate the United States? Well, since the Russian Revolution in 1917 when the U.S. supported the anti communist side, Russia and the US have been in a fairly constant state of tension. Numerous territorial encroachment, proxy wars, and alternating alliances have set the stages for both countries to fear each other's imperialist goals. In recent years, Russian President Vladimir Putin has called the United States a parasite, living off the global economy. Throughout Russia, Americans are given the nickname "pindos" that suggested that they are heavily armed and surrounded by technology but weak and ineffectual without it. This break in relations can in part be attributed to the US's push for sanctions following Russia's annexation of Crimea. A number of problems with Russia's economy, including the collapse of their currency and their inability to borrow money are the result of US involvement. Amongst Russian citizens, prices for food and basic goods have dramatically increased. Last year, Russia's economy grew barely half a percent, compared to 4.5% in 2010. Russia is also majorly unhappy with the buildup of NATO forces throughout Eastern Europe following the collapse of Soviet Union. They see the increased in military bases and personnel as a method of keeping Russia subjugated. There is a considerate amount of propaganda coming from both Russia stated controlled media sources and long held conspiratorial beliefs about the United States. Many Russians believe that the events of 9/11 was planned by US government in order to invade the Middle East. And roughly 40% of the Russians don't believe that the US ever even landed on the moon. Analysts have also said that Russian hatred of the US is calculated to strengthen Russian foreign policy. In situations like the 2008 South Ossetia war, Russian accused US of supporting the genocide of Ossetians. However, numerous reports claimed that Russia started the conflict themselves. Russia also said that the 2013 Euromaidan protests in the Kiev before the annexation of Crimea were orchestrated by American forces and not simple local civil unrest. As a direct representation of East meets with the West ideological and political disagreements, the US and Russia are both vying for greater influence. This divide has made Russia an even more vilified figure around the world than the US. A recent pew poll has found that nearly every country has a very low confidence in Vladimir Putin with most negative ratings passing 75%. Even in the Middle East, President Brack Obama polled with a higher favorability than Putin. So why does Russia hate the US? A mix of historical tension, political rivalry, cultural clash, sanctions and heavy propaganda have all made for an extremely hostile situation.

In July 2015, Greece voted against further austerity measures in exchange for bailing out their tremendous debt. This move has continued to strain the relationship between Greece and Germany as a two major players in the EU's debt crisis. But this isn't the first time the two countries have come head to head. So why do Greece and Germany hate each other? The two country's difficult relationship can actually be traced back to modern Greece's beginnings. In the 1830s, Greece finally established itself as independent from the Ottoman Empire. The first ruler was Otto from Bavaria, a German State. However Otto was still a teenager at the time, so Greece was actually ruled by three other Bavarians, who were not welcomed by the Greeks. This eventually led to King Otto's deposition and the Queen's near assassination. This rocky start didn't bode well for the future of their relationship. Fast forward to World War II, when Hitler invaded Greece in 1941, the following German occupation led to hundreds of thousands dying of hunger or being murdered. Over million Greeks were made homeless and Greece's banks were drained to fund the war. In 1944, German soldiers massacred over 200 Greeks in retaliation for the deaths of seven Nazi soldiers. Greece's grievances concerning this event have continued till today. In 1960, Germany paid toughly 6 million Euros as war reparations and said they owned them no more. Greece passionately objected to closing the issue and the debate continued for decades. In 1997, a Greek court found that Germany was responsible for further compensation for 1944 massacre. However, in 2012, the Hague ruled that German was immune from foreign lawsuits, sparking the ire of Greek citizens. Today the two countries continue to be at odds over the money Greece owes its creditors. The Greek Prime Minister argued that the amount of money due to them reparations would cover a significant portion of the debt in question. Greece has threatened to seize German property to pay for the alleged reparations. Meanwhile, Germany and the rest of the euro zone are desperate to find a solution that keeps the EU economy from collapsing from Greece's inflexibility. The two countries have intense history that is doing them no favors in calming the waters.

- **Compound Dictation Two**

The Gua Sha Treatment

Q (Mr. Quinlin): These accusations are incredibly ridiculous and laughable.

W (woman from the Child Welfare Agency): Perhaps you don't understand your friend. According to the doctor's report, the condition and coloration of the bruises when afflicted two days prior to Danis' head injury, we believe these photographs have sufficient evidence to demonstrate Danis Xu lives in dangerous home environment and should remain under the protection of the State.

J (judge): Please return to your seats.

Q: How could you do this to your son? Is this something you forgot to make me know? You know that no one will notice your son's back. It's like roasted beef.

X (Xu Datong): That is Gua sha, a traditional Chinese medical treatment. Danis had a stomachache that day and Gua sha is simple a cure, a home remedy you call it. I had this on me endless time when I as a kid.

Q: If you call it some kind of treatment, what do you see to consider child abuse?

J: If you two want to chitchat, we can all go home. Does the defense have something more to add?

W: No.

X: Yes, I do. I think you don't understand .You know Gua sha is a traditional Chinese medical treatment used for nearly all kinds of illness. For thousands of years, Chinese medicine recognized that there are seven "Jing" and eight "Mai". An example, it's like small streams that run into rivers and then into seas. A person's body has an invisible but very complex system of vessel network just like the computer network and also, the human "Qi" from Tan tien finally goes through Tan tien. It's the same principle.

J: He's your client. What did he say? Western mind doesn't understand what you said. Perhaps try another way, Mr. Xu. What does it say on every Missouri license plate?

X: "Show Me State".

J: Precisely! Can you get an authoritative medical expert to make your testimony in plain English that a country judge can understand?

X: Yes, I can try.

P (Prosecutor): All right, Mr Quinlin. Let's get straight to the point, shall we? Mr Xu is an employee of Meantime New Media and also your best friend, right?

Q (Mr. Quinlin): Yes, he is an employee and I am proud to call Mr Xu my friend.

P: In what sort of business is Meantime New Media engaged?

Q: We design and distribute video games.

P: Quite true. You are known in your industry for the cutting-edge technology and high quality crafts. And I happen to have some of your games…

Q: What a coincidence.

P: "Death Quest", "Hell Races", "Malcolm's Massacre".

Q: We also created "Dream Seekers", "The Sally Says. Educational Series".

P: But you were taken by concerned citizens' protest against excessively violent contents in your goals, were you?

Q: Those groups target all the video game designers.

P: That maybe. But Meantime New Media consistently in industry leagued in violence complaints, I also have a few video captured scenes from some of your most popular games. The graphics are astonishingly realistic. Like this "Guardian of the Universe" character, who punches his fist straight through his enemy's chest. And this one, when the hero delivers a single kick, his enemy's head splits open, brains oozing out.

J: Is this charming little show going anywhere?

P: Who created and designed these images?

Q: Video game design is a collective activity.

P: Yes, but someone has to initiate the creative vision for the game. Yes, someone recently received an award for his video game design, especially for his design of a violent all-powerful monkey. And that someone would be…

Q: Datong Xu.

P: If you may take one look at the work Datong Xu is engaged in day in and day out, you see this is a man steep in the culture of violence.

X: Culture of violence? The character in my latest video is adapted from ancient Chinese storyteller. Sun Wukong (monkey king) is a good-hearted and compassionate hero. He represent our traditional values and ethics.

P: Oh, traditional values and ethics, Mr. Xu?

W: Burton, you don't have to play our part.

P: We do, if we want to hit a home run, sweetheart.

P: Now I read *Journey to the West* in English, the book this character is drawn from. Here is the story where peaches that take nine thousand years to harvest are our entrusted to Sun Wukong. Yet this typical Chinese monkey appropriated the entire harvest for himself. And when the poor farmers resist him, he totally destroyed their orchard…Here is another example of this creature's value system. A certain fairy creates the pill of eternal youth. Not only is this odd Sun Wukong consuming the entire pills and not leave it for anyone else, but he also overturns the furnace and destroys the workshop that take millennium to construct.

X: That's nonsense!

P: Now it's such an obstreperous rude Chinese monkey. It's what Mr. Xu refers to as examples of values and morals.

X: What do you think what you are? You know nothing about Chinese culture!

D (Doctor): Gua sha, has a history of more than two thousand years in China. In most cases, illness that acupuncture and message are able to treat can be helped with Gua sha as well. Gua sha work according to the thermal dynamical principle that heat opens, cold closes. Does it hurt?

Q (Mr. Quinlin): Well, not.

D: With Gua sha, you can open up the blood capillary. How does it feel now?

Q: A little bit hot.

D: Hence, Gua sha is able to stimulate and increase the volume and flow of blood cells, which is beneficial to the blood circulation, and has a health, restoring effect of reestablishing body's nature by biological circulation. All right, all done. Why don't you have a look in the mirror? You will not consider that abuse, won't you?

Q: I understand now. Thank you so much, doctor.

- *Video Appreciation: Understanding the Rise of China*

The world is changing with really remarkable speed. If you look at the chart at the top here, you'll see that in 2025, these Goldman Sachs projections suggest that the Chinese economy will be almost the same size as the American economy. And if you look at the chart for 2050, it's projected that the Chinese economy will be twice the size of the American economy, and the Indian economy will be almost the same size as the American economy. And we should bear in mind here that these projections were drawn up before the Western financial crisis.

A couple of weeks ago, I was looking at the latest projection by BNP Paribas for when China will have a larger economy than the United States. Goldman Sachs projected 2027. The post-crisis projection is 2020. That's just a decade away. China is going to change the world in two fundamental respects. First of all, it's a huge developing country with a population of 1.3 billion people, which has been growing for over 30 years at around 10 percent a year.

And within a decade, it will have the largest economy in the world. Never before in the modern era has the largest economy in the world been that of a developing country, rather than a developed country. Secondly, for the first time in the modern era, the dominant country in the world — which I think is what China will become—will be not from the West and from very, very different civilizational roots.

Now I know it's a widespread assumption in the West that, as countries modernize, they also Westernize. This is an illusion. It's an assumption that modernity is a product simply of competition, markets and technology. It is not; it is also shaped equally by history and culture. China is not like the West, and it will not become like the West. It will remain in very fundamental respects very different. Now the big question here is obviously, how do we make sense of China? How do we try to understand what China is? And the problem we have in the

West at the moment by-and-large is that the conventional approach is that we understand it really in Western terms, using Western ideas. We can't. Now I want to offer you three building blocks for trying to understand what China is like—just as a beginning.

The first is this, that China is not really a nation state. Okay, it's called itself a nation state for the last hundred years. But everyone who knows anything about China knows it's a lot older than this. This was what China looked like with the victory of the Qin Dynasty in 221 B.C. at the end of the warring state period—the birth of modern China. And you can see it against the boundaries of modern China. Or immediately afterward, the Han Dynasty, still 2,000 years ago. And you can see already it occupies most of what we now know as Eastern China, which is where the vast majority of Chinese lived then and live now.

Now what is extraordinary about this is, what gives China it's sense of being China, what gives the Chinese the sense of what it is to be Chinese, comes not from the last hundred years, not from the nation state period, which is what happened in the West, but from the period, if you like, of the civilization state. I'm thinking here, for example, of customs like ancestral worship, of a very distinctive notion of the state, likewise, a very distinctive notion of the family, social relationships like guanxi, Confucian values and so on. These are all things that come from the period of the civilization state. In other words, China, unlike the Western states and most countries in the world, is shaped by its sense of civilization, its existence as a civilization state, rather than as a nation state. And there's one other thing to add to this, and that is this: Of course we know China's big, huge, demographically and geographically, with a population of 1.3 billion people. What we often aren't really aware of is the fact that China is extremely diverse and very pluralistic, and in many ways very decentralized. You can't run a place on this scale simply from Beijing, even though we think this to be the case. It's never been the case.

So this is China, a civilization state, rather than a nation state. And what does it mean? Well I think it has all sorts of profound implications. I'll give you two quick ones. The first is that the most important political value for the Chinese is unity, is the maintenance of Chinese civilization. You know, 2,000 years ago, Europe: breakdown, the fragmentation of the Holy Roman Empire [Roman Empire]. It divided, and it's remained divided ever since. China, over the same time period, went in exactly the opposite direction, very painfully holding this huge civilization, civilization state together.

The second is maybe more prosaic, which is Hong Kong. Do you remember the handover of Hong Kong by Britain to China in 1997? You may remember what the Chinese constitutional proposition was. One country, two systems. And I'll lay a wager that barely anyone in the West believed them. "Window dressing. When China gets it's hands on Hong Kong, that won't be the case." 13 years on, the political and legal system in Hong Kong is as different now as it was in 1997. We were wrong. Why were we wrong? We were wrong because we thought, naturally enough, in nation state ways. Think of German unification, 1990. What happened? Well, basically the East was swallowed by the West. One nation, one system. That is the nation state mentality. But you can't run a country like China, a civilization state, on the basis of one civilization, one system. It doesn't work. So actually the response of China to the question of Hong Kong—as it will be to the question of Taiwan — was a natural response: one civilization, many systems.

Let me offer you another building block to try and understand China—maybe not such a comfortable one. The Chinese have a very, very different conception of race to most other countries. Do you know, of the 1.3 billion Chinese, over 90 percent of them think they belong to the same race, the Han. Now this is completely different from the other world's most populous countries. India, the United States, Indonesia, Brazil—all of them are multiracial. The Chinese don't feel like that. China is only multiracial really at the margins. So the question is, why? Well the reason, I think, essentially is, again, back to the civilization state. A history of at least 2,000 years, a history of conquest, occupation, absorption, assimilation and so on, led to the process by which, over time, this notion of the Han emerged—of course, nurtured by a growing and very powerful sense of cultural identity.

Now the great advantage of this historical experience has been that, without the Han, China could never have held together. The Han identity has been the cement which has held this country together. The great disadvantage of it is that the Han have a very weak conception of cultural difference. They really believe in their own superiority, and they are disrespectful of those who are not. Hence their attitude, for example, to the Uyghurs and to the Tibetans.

Or let me give you my third building block, the Chinese state. Now the relationship between the state and society in China is very different from that in the West. Now we in the West overwhelmingly seem to think—in these days at least—that the authority and legitimacy of the state is a function of democracy. The problem with this proposition is that the Chinese state enjoys more legitimacy and more authority amongst the Chinese than is true with any Western state. And the reason for this is because—well, there are two reasons, I think. And it's obviously got nothing to do with democracy, because in our terms the Chinese certainly don't have a democracy. And the reason for this is, firstly, because the state in China is given a very special— it enjoys a very special significance as the representative, the embodiment and the guardian of Chinese civilization, of the civilization state. This is as close as China gets to a kind of spiritual role.

And the second reason is because, whereas in Europe and North America, the state's power is continuously challenged—I mean in the European tradition, historically against the church, against other sectors of the aristocracy, against merchants and so on—for 1,000 years, the power of the Chinese state has not been challenged. It's had no serious rivals. So you can see that the way in which power has been constructed in China is very different from our experience in Western history. The result, by the way, is that the Chinese have a very different view of the state. Whereas we tend to view it as an intruder, a stranger, certainly an organ whose powers need to be limited or defined and constrained, the Chinese don't see the state like that at all. The Chinese view the state as an intimate—not just as an intimate actually, as a member of the family—not just in fact as a member of the family, but as the head of the family, the patriarch of the family. This is the Chinese view of the state—very, very different to ours. It's embedded in society in a different kind of way to what is the case in the West.

And I would suggest to you that actually what we are dealing with here, in the Chinese context, is a new kind of paradigm, which is different from anything we've had to think about in the past. Know that China believes in the market and the state. I mean, Adam Smith, already writing in the late 18th century said, "The Chinese market is larger and more developed and more sophisticated than anything in Europe." And, apart from the Mao period, that has remained more-or-less the case ever since. But this is combined with an extremely strong and ubiquitous state. The state is everywhere in China. I mean, it's leading firms, many of them are still publicly owned. Private firms, however large they are, like Lenovo, depend in many ways on state patronage. Targets for the economy and so on are set by the state. And the state, of course, its authority flows into lots of other areas—as we are familiar with—with something like the one-child policy.

Moreover, this is a very old state tradition, a very old tradition of statecraft. I mean, if you want an illustration of this, the Great Wall is one. But this is another, this is the Grand Canal, which was constructed in the first instance in the fifth century B.C. and was finally completed in the seventh century A.D. It went for 1,114 miles, linking Beijing with Hangzhou and Shanghai. So there's a long history of extraordinary state infrastructural projects in China, which I suppose helps us to explain what we see today, which is something like the Three Gorges Dam and many other expressions of state competence within China. So there we have three building blocks for trying to to understand the difference that is China—the civilization state, the notion of race and the nature of the state and its relationship to society.

And yet we still insist, by-and-large, in thinking that we can understand China by simply drawing on Western experience, looking at it through Western eyes, using Western concepts. If you want to know why we unerringly seem to get China wrong—our predictions about what's going to happen to China are incorrect—this is the reason. Unfortunately I think, I have to say that I think attitude towards China is that of a kind of little Westerner mentality. It's kind of arrogant. It's arrogant in the sense that we think that we are best, and therefore we have the universal measure. And secondly, it's ignorant. We refuse to really address the issue of difference. You know, there's a very interesting passage in a book by Paul Cohen, the American historian. And Paul Cohen argues that the West thinks of itself as probably the most cosmopolitan of all cultures. But it's not. In many ways, it's the most parochial, because for 200 years, the West has been so dominant in the world that it's not really needed to understand other cultures, other civilizations. Because, at the end of the day, it could, if necessary by force, get its own way. Whereas those cultures—virtually the rest of the world, in fact—which have been in a far weaker position, vis-a-vis the West, have been thereby forced to understand the West, because of the

West's presence in those societies. And therefore, they are, as a result, more cosmopolitan in many ways than the West.

I mean, take the question of East Asia. East Asia: Japan, Korea, China, etc.—a third of the world's population lives there, now the largest economic region in the world. And I'll tell you now, that East Asianers, people from East Asia, are far more knowledgeable about the West than the West is about East Asia. Now this point is very germane, I'm afraid, to the present. Because what's happening? Back to that chart at the beginning—the Goldman Sachs chart. What is happening is that, very rapidly in historical terms, the world is being driven and shaped, not by the old developed countries, but by the developing world. We've seen this in terms of the G20 —usurping very rapidly the position of the G7, or the G8. And there are two consequences of this. First, the West is rapidly losing its influence in the world. There was a dramatic illustration of this actually a year ago—Copenhagen, climate change conference. Europe was not at the final negotiating table. When did that last happen? I would wager it was probably about 200 years ago. And that is what is going to happen in the future.

And the second implication is that the world will inevitably, as a consequence, become increasingly unfamiliar to us, because it'll be shaped by cultures and experiences and histories that we are not really familiar with, or conversant with. And at last, I'm afraid—take Europe, America is slightly different—but Europeans by and large, I have to say, are ignorant, are unaware about the way the world is changing. Some people—I've got an English friend in China, and he said, "The continent is sleepwalking into oblivion." Well, maybe that's true, maybe that's an exaggeration. But there's another problem which goes along with this—that Europe is increasingly out of touch with the world—and that is a sort of loss of a sense of the future. I mean, Europe once, of course, once commanded the future in it's confidence. Take the 19th century for example. But this, alas, is no longer true.

If you want to feel the future, if you want to taste the future, try China—there's old Confucius. This is a railway station the like of which you've never seen before. It doesn't even look like a railway station. This is the new Guangzhou railway station for the high-speed trains. China already has a bigger network than any other country in the world and will soon have more than all the rest of the world put together. Or take this: Now this is an idea, but it's an idea to by tried out shortly in a suburb of Beijing. Here you have a megabus, on the upper deck carries about 2,000 people. It travels on rails down a suburban road, and the cars travel underneath it. And it does speeds of up to about 100 miles an hour. Now this is the way things are going to move, because China has a very specific problem, which is different from Europe and different from the United States. China has huge numbers of people and no space. So this is a solution to a situation where China's going to have many, many, many cities over 20 million people.

Okay, so how would I like to finish? Well, what should our attitude be towards this world that we see very rapidly developing before us? I think there will be good things about it and there will be bad things about it. But I want to argue, above all, a big picture positive for this world. For 200 years, the world was essentially governed by a fragment of the human population. That's what Europe and North America represented. The arrival of countries like China and India— between them 38 percent of the world's population—and others like Indonesia and Brazil and so on, represent the most important single act of democratization in the last 200 years. Civilizations and cultures, which had been ignored, which had no voice, which were not listened to, which were not known about, will have a different sort of representation in this world. As humanists, we must welcome, surely, this transformation. And we will have to learn about these civilizations.

This big ship here was the one sailed in by Zheng He in the early 15th century on his great voyages around the South China Sea, the East China Sea and across the Indian Ocean to East Africa. The little boat in front of it was the one in which, 80 years later, Christopher Columbus crossed the Atlantic. (Laughter) Or, look carefully at this silk scroll made by Zhu Zhou in 1368. I think they're playing golf. Christ, the Chinese even invented golf.

Welcome to the future. Thank you.

◇ Section A

- **Conversation One**

M: So, what's the next thing on the agenda, Mary?

W: Well, it's the South Theater Company. They want to know if we'd be interested in sponsoring a tour they want to make to East Asia.

M: East Asia? Uh... and how much are they hoping to get from us?

W: Well, the letter mentions 20,000 pounds, but I don't know if they might settle for less.

M: Do they say what they would cover? Have they anything specific in mind?

W: No, I think they are just asking all the firms in town for as much money as they think they'll give.

M: And we are worth 20,000 pounds, right?

W: It seems so.

M: Very flattering. But I am not awfully happy with the idea. What do we get out of it?

W: Oh, good publicity I suppose. So what I suggest is not that we just give them a sum of money, but that we offer to pay for something specific like travel or something, and that in return, we ask for our name to be printed prominently in the program, and that they give us free advertising space in it.

M: But the travel bill would be enormous, and we could never manage that.

W: I know. But why don't we offer to pay for the printing of the programs ourselves on condition that on the front cover there's something like "This program is presented with the compliments of Norland Electronics", and free advertising of course.

M: Good idea. Well, let's get back to them and ask what the program they want will cost. Then we can see if we are interested or not.

Questions 1 to 4 are based on the conversation you have just heard.

1. What do we learn about the South Theater Company?

2. How much does the South Theater Company ask for in the letter?

3. What benefit does the woman say their firm can get by sponsoring the South Theater Company?

4. What does the woman suggest they do instead of paying the South Theater Company's travel expenses?

- **Conversation Two**

W: Rock stars now face a new hazard—voice abuse. After last week's announcement that Phil Collins might give up touring because live concerts are ruining his voice, doctors are counseling stars about the dos and don5ts of voice care. Here in the studio today, we have Mr. Paul Philips, an expert from the High field Hospital. Paul, what advice would you give to singers facing voice problems?

M: If pop singers have got voice problems, they really need to be more selective about where they work. They shouldn't work in smoky atmospheres. They also need to think about resting their voices after a show. Something else they need to be careful about is medicines, aspirin, for example. Singers should avoid aspirin. It thins the blood. And if a singer coughs, this can result in the bruising of the vocal chords.

W: And is it true that some singers use drugs before concerts to boost their voices when they have voice problems?

M: Yes, this does happen on occasion. They are easily-available on the Continent and they are useful if a singer has problems with his vocal chords and has to sing that night. But if they are taken regularly, they cause a thinning of the voice muscle. Most pop singers suffer from three things: lack of training, overuse and abuse of the voice, especially when they are young. They have difficult lives. When they go on tour, they do a vast number of concerts, sing in smoky places.

W: So, what would you advise these singers to do?

M: Warm you voice up before a show and warm it down after.

Questions 5 to 8 are based on the conversation you have just heard.

5. What does last week's announcement say about rock star Phil Collins?

6. What does Paul Philips say about aspirin?

7. What does Paul Philips say about young pop singers?

8. What are the speakers mainly talking about?

◈ **Section B**

- **Passage One**

Would you trust a robot to park your car? The question will confront New Yorkers in

February as the city's first robotic parking opens in Chinatown. The technology has been successfully applied overseas, but the only other public robotic garage in the United States has been troublesome, dropping vehicles and trapping cars because of technical problems.

Nonetheless, the developers of the Chinatown garage are confident with the technology and are counting on it to squeeze 67 cars in an apartment-building basement that would otherwise fit only 24, accomplished by removing a maneuver space normally required.

A human-shaped robot won't be stepping into your car to drive it.
Rather, the garage itself does the parking. The driver stops the car on a flat platform and gets out. The platform is lowered into the garage, and it is then transported to a vacant parking space by a computer-controlled device similar to an elevator that also runs sideways.

There is no human supervision, but an attendant will be on hand to accept cash and explain the system to new users.

Parking rates will be attracted about $400 monthly or $25 per day, according to Ari Milstein, the director of planning for Automation Parking Systems, which is the U.S. subsidiary of a German company. This company has built automated garages in several countries overseas and in the United States for residents of a Washington, D.C. apartment building.

Questions 9 to 12 are based on the passage you have just heard

9. What do we learn about robotic parking in the U.S. so far?

10. advantage does robotic parking have according to its developers?

11. What does the attendant do in the automated garage?

12. What does the company say about the parking rates?

• **Passage Two**

Alcoholism is a serious disease. Nearly nine million Americans alone suffer from the illness. Many scientists disagree about what the differences are between an alcohol addict and a social drinker. The difference occurs when someone needs to drink. And this need gets in the way of his health or behavior.

Alcohol causes a loss of judgment and alertness. After a long period, alcoholism can deteriorate the liver, the brain and other parts of the body. The illness is dangerous, because it is involved in half of all automobile accidents. Another problem is that the victim often denies being an alcohol addict and won't get help.

Solutions do exist. Many hospitals and centers help patients cope. Without assistance, the victim can destroy his life. He would detach himself from the routines of life. He may lose his employment, home or loved ones.

All the causes of the sickness are not discovered yet. There is no standard for a person with alcoholism. Victims range in age, race, sex and background. Some groups of people are more vulnerable to the illness. People from broken homes and North American Indians are two examples. People from broken homes often lack stable lives. Indians likewise had their traditional life taken from them by white settlers who often encourage them to consume alcohol to prevent them from fighting back. The problem has now been passed on.

Alcoholism is clearly present in society today. People have started to get help and information. With proper assistance, victims can put their lives together one day.

Questions 13 to 15 are based on the passage you have just heard

13. What is the problem of the victims about alcoholism according to the speaker?

14. Why did white settlers introduce alcohol to Indians?

15. What does the speaker seem to believe about those affected by alcoholism?

◇ Section C

- **Recording One**

Hi, everybody. On Tuesday, America went to the polls. And the message you sent was clear: you voted for action, not politics as usual.

You elected us to focus on your jobs, not ours. That's why I've invited leaders of both parties to the White House next week, so we can start to build consensus around challenges we can only solve together.

I also intend to bring in business, labor and civic leaders from around the country from outside Washington to get their ideas and input as well.

At a time when our economy is still recovering from the Great Recession, our top priority has to be jobs and growth. That's the focus of the plan I talked about throughout the campaign.

It's a plan to reward businesses that create jobs here in America, and give people access to the education and training that those businesses are looking for.

It's a plan to rebuild our infrastructure and keep us on the cutting edge of innovation and clean energy.

And it's a plan to reduce our deficit in a balanced and responsible way.

This is even more important because at the end of this year, we face a series of deadlines that require us to make major decisions about how to pay down our deficit — decisions that will have a huge impact on the economy and the middle class, not only now but in the future.

Last year, I worked with Democrats and Republicans to cut a trillion dollars, worth of spending, and I intend to work with both parties to do more.

But as I said over and over again on the campaign trail, we can't just cut our way to prosperity.

If we're serious about reducing the deficit, we have to combine spending cuts with revenue — and that means asking the wealthiest Americans to pay a little more in taxes.

That's how we did it when Bill Clinton was President.

And that's the only way we can afford to invest in education and job training and manufacturing—all the ingredients of a strong middle class and a strong economy.

Already, I've put forward a detailed plan that allows us to make these investments while reducing our deficit by \$4 trillion over the next decade.

Questions 16 to 19 are based on the recording you have just heard.

16. Why are leaders of both parties invited to the White House next week?

17. `What is the focus of the mentioned plan?

18. What are the major decisions about?

19. What does combining spending cuts with revenue mean?

• Recording Two

Most people agree that eating healthy food is important. But sometimes making good food choices can be tough. Now, there are apps that can help people learn about the food they eat to improve their diets and their dining out experience.

OpenTable

OpenTable helps people choose restaurants when they want to go out to eat. OpenTable is a free service that shows users restaurant availability based on where and when they want to dine. OpenTable users can also make restaurant reservations directly through the app or website. OpenTable gives users points when they make reservations. The points can add up to discounts on restaurant visits.

When users make reservations through OpenTable they get an email confirmation. They can also add the reservation directly to their electronic calendar.

Max McCalman's Cheese and Wine

But which wines go best with which cheeses? Max McCalman's Cheese and Wine App can help. It provides information about hundreds of different cheeses and suggests wines to pair with each. More than 3,000 possible combinations can be found based on 600 different cheeses. The app includes a "Cheese 101" section that teaches the basics about choosing a cheese. Max McCalman's Cheese & Wine Pairing App is free for iPhone and iPad.

Epicurious

Epicurious is a free app and website to help users find recipes and become better cooks. The app has more than 30, 000 recipes and can create a shopping list based on the ingredients in a recipe. Users can search by ingredients or buy vegetables that are in season where they live. The app also rates recipes for popularity and other qualities. Users also provide advice about making the recipes. Each recipe has a list of ingredients, preparation time, instructions as well as a photo of the finished meal.

Calorific

What does 200 calories look like? It can be hard to picture. For example, 200 calories of broccoli and 200 calories of cake look very different! The app Calorific shows just that. Calorific provides images of 200 calories worth of food. The pictures can help people on diets and those who just want to eat healthier. The app also provides the weights of each food pictured. The app is free for iPad and iPhone. There is also a version that provides more information for a price.

Harvest

An app called Harvest informs users about seasonal fruits and vegetables in different areas. This can be helpful in planning meals. Harvest also tells about pesticide use and organic food. Users can learn the best ways to safely store food and keep it fresh longer.

Questions 20 to 22 are based on the recording you have just heard.

20. What are the points Open Table offers users for?

21. What do we learn about Epicurious?

22. How does Calorific help people get healthier?

• **Recording Three**

We've had fifty years of progress since that landmark Surgeon General's report back in 1964. Over these years incredible things have taken place. Our society has changed — changed in terms of tobacco use, in terms of its acceptance of smoking in public establishments, in restaurants, in bars. So things have really changed for the better. In addition, smoking rates have come down in the United States.

We went from 43 percent of adult smokers in the United States to 18 percent currently. So that's really made incredible headway, yet I have to emphasize the battle isn't over, the war isn't over.

Eighteen percent of American adults who are still smoking, basically 40 million people in our population. That being said we have to realize also that of that whole group, we're going to have roughly a half million people every year dying from smoking related diseases.

So although we've made progress in a half century, the reality is we still have a lot of work to do. So, you know, we increasingly see tough advertisements on the air against smoking.

These ads are working. In particular, the CDC — the Center for Disease Control and Prevention came up with a series of advertisements from former smokers called TIPS.

And that really was quite effective in terms of reducing the number of smokers. In addition, there's various policies that need to be implemented and further implemented in order to make us a tobacco-free society.

So we really have to work at the idea of using media, using those advertisements. We have to look at really concentrating on the youth of America to make it more difficult to actually get cigarettes. And in addition we have to look at the idea of pricing cigarettes appropriately so that ultimately it becomes a hardship to use those products.

So, let's talk a little bit about packaging those products. Other countries have much more graphic detail of the potential dangers of smoking.

We're currently working closely; the office of the Surgeon General is working closely with the Food and Drug Administration, specifically the Center for Tobacco Products and are reanalyzing the whole row of the idea of the warning labels and the idea of how graphic they should be, and so there will probably be more information coming out on this in the near future.

Questions 23 to 25 are based on the recording you have just heard.

23. What is the number of smokers in America?

24. What measures can be taken to make it harder to get cigarettes?

25. What institution does the speaker most likely come from?

■ Chapter 4

· Compound Dictation One

All the Backstory for "Avengers: Age of Ultron" in 7 minutes

Avenger's age of ultron is the 11th movie set in the so called Marvel cinematic universe. That shared universe also include: 62 television episodes, 31 comic book titles and five DVD only short films. Holy living… is that there is a lot of lead up, but don't worry, we'll tell you all this stuff you actually need to know to be ready for this latest hyper mega super ultra blockbuster.

It all began in the first iron man movie where we meet Tony Stark, a weapon's designer with a raging libido and a computer butler named Jarvis. He's a genius and also a complete prick. After getting captured and gravely injured by terrorists in Afghanistan, he builds a robot suit out of a spare parts and returns to the US. He decides he doesn't like weapons manufacturing, builds a better version of his suit, saves southern California from another guy in a robot suit and tells the world he's decided to be a real life superhero. Right after that, he's approached by a guy named Nick Fury who runs a covert military operation called SHIELD. He says there are secret superheroes around the world and he's putting together a team of them. What will they be avenging? Who knows? But they have another recruit in mind. Bruce Banner a.k.a, the incredible hulk, whom we meet in … well The Incredible Hulk. Bruce was a wimpy scientist working with the US government who was tricked into participating in a military experiment that gave him unwanted power. When he gets angry or excited, he turns into a big dumb green rage monster. After some explosiony hygienes, Bruce goes into hiding and learns to control his powers through meditations and stuff. Don't worry too much about Iron Man 2. The only things to know about it are that Tony became a global superstar as Iron Man. He meets a SHILED super spy named Natasha Rimanov, a.k.a. black widow. And he has a complicated relationship with a military dude named James Rhodes. Rhody is a long time friend but thinks Tony needs to cooperate more with the government. He also has some of his own robot armor. They call him War Machine, but it's not nearly as colorful. Then we got the first Thor movie, hoo boy this one is a mind bender. We meet Thor, a warrior prince from an extra dimensional planetoid called Azgard, which is populated by near immortal beings who used to visit earth. When Oden time, humans thought of them as gods. Thor is very strong. He uses a magic hammer that can only be held by those that the hammer deems worthy. He has an evil brother named Loki. He has a scientist love interest in Jane. And he is aided by the helpful god Hamdo. Thor and Loki get into a Titanic tassel and Thor wins. He encountered a SHILED agent called Clinton Barton a.k.a. hawk guy who only uses bows and arrows for some reason. We also meet a good guy astrophysicist named Erik Selvic who get secret mind controlled by Loki before Nick Fury recruited him to work for SHILD. Captain America the first avenger is a flash back but a very important one. Meet Steve Rogers a scrawny weakling in the 1940s who volunteers for a military experiment that makes him super strong and they gave him a super power shield made of ultra rare mineral Vibranium. After spending some time entertaining audiences as a propaganda tool named Captain America, he becomes a legit soldier doing secret missions against the science obsessed Nazi splinter group called hydra. He stops a big evil hydra plan but seemingly dies while crash landing into some very cold snow. This is very sad for his war buddy and sorta girl friend Peggy Carter. But fear not, we find out that he just got frozen and was discovered in the present where he's sought out and recruited by… you guessed it! Nick Fury! You know what that means. It's time for the first avengers movie!

Loki comes to earth with a super powered soul controlling staff, steals a magic cube and uses it to launch a plan for world domination. Nick Fury rounds up all the super heroes we've already met, sensitive Steve, cool Clint, total dick Tony, thunderous Thor and nasty Natasha who sent to recruit blister out Bruce. They become SHILD'S first, last and only line of defense against Loki's extra dimensional invaders. They become…the avengers! After some squalling and mind control, sorry Hawk guy, they get together and defeated the bad guy during a big fat battle in New York City where Iron Man fights a big fat space snake! Then they get some shawarma, hmmm, shawarma. Oh one quick thing, we also learn that Natasha used to work for the Russians but doesn't anymore. You can basically ignore Iron Man Three except you should know that Tony creates a bunch of remote controlled robot suits he calls the Iron Legion and meanwhile entrusts his company to capable girlfriend Pepper Props. And you can mostly ignore Thor, the dark world, aside from one notable item that pros up, a powerful space goo called the ether. This thing holds one of the six infinity stones, back in the avengers Loki had two other infinity stones. And an evil space lord named Fanos wanted to collect them all. Ok enough weird space mystical stuff. Let's talk about Captain America, the winter soldier. SHIELD is riding high after saving the world and cap is their poster child. But SHIELD is up to some questionable business. They're building a world wide monitoring system that can kill basically everybody. Nick Fury seems fine with this plan until he is attacked and framed as a traitor and it turns out SHIELD has been taken over by…HYDRA. Cap goes on a run with Natasha and his new friend Falcon who is a war vet with a flying machine. They link up with a SHIELD officer named Maria Hill and the disgraced Nick Fury who has faked his own death to go undercover. Cap goes all Ed Snowden on everybody and tells the world about the evil inside SHIELD. The world's governments decide to force it to disband, so bye bye SHIELD. You can mostly ignore Guardians of the Galaxy because as fun as it is, it takes place like a bijulion miles away in space and has no avengers in it. The only thing you need to know is that another infinity stones popped up in that one and Thanos really wanted it. Ok, last thing I promise, we have briefly met a pair of twins named Pietro and Wonda Maximoff. According to an obscure tie in comic they're angry activists from a war torn European country called Sokovia. They want to over throw their shitty government. So they volunteer for a Hydra program run by a dude named Baron Struker. The program gave them super powers, so now Pieto can run really fast and Wonda can do weird stuff with her mind. We see them at a short scene at the end of Winter Soldier imprisoned by Hydra and not looking happy about it. And now you are ready to see Avengers: Age of Ultron, which will have approximately 8000 characters, 4 million different locations and 12 billion sequels. Here's hoping our brains don't melt.

- **Compound Dictation Two**

The US Sub-prime Crisis

Meet Uncle Sam. He has a lot of bills to pay, almost $ 4 trillion worth every year. Uncle Sam's income is a little over $ 2 trillion per year. To make up the difference, the deficit, he does what most Americans do. He borrows money. When Uncle Sam takes out a loan, he calls it a bond. Bonds can be held by banks, investors or even foreign governments. Uncle Sam has to promise to pay interest on these bonds just as you do on any loan you take out. Ever think about paying your mortgage with your credit card? That's exactly what Uncle Sam does. He takes out new loans, new bonds, so that he can make payments on the old ones. All those loans and especially all that interest adds up. Right now, Uncle Sam owes about $14 trillion. To put that in perspective, $14 trillion is about the same as the national GDP, the total value of all the goods and services produced by the American economy in an entire year. It's such a huge amount of money that Uncle Sam is starting to run out of people to borrow from. And he's having trouble just paying the interest on his loans. The obvious solution would be to either cut spending or increase taxes. But if he cuts spending, the people that he's spending money on would complain that they don't have money to spend and that he was hurting the economy. If he tries to raise taxes enough to close this gap, not only would people definitely have less money to spend, he'd probably have riots on his hands. So Uncle Sam chooses the easy way to make money. Just make it. He calls up the Federal Reserve, which is our central bank and like magic, dollars are created and deposited in banks all around America. The problem is if there are more of something there is, the less it's worth. The same goes for the U.S. dollar. The more dollars there are, the less each one will buy. That's why commodities like gasoline, food and gold become more expensive when Uncle Sam does his money-making magic. The commodities aren't really worth more, your money is just worth less. That's called inflation. Remember the foreign governments that lent money to Uncle Sam? When they lent money to the American government, something interesting happened. It made the U.S. look richer, and their countries looked poorer. When a country looks poorer compared to America, one dollar of our money buys a lot of their money, so they can pay their workers only a few pennies a day. With such low labor costs, they can sell their products in America for lower prices than any American manufacturer can. The easiest way for American companies to compete is to move their factories overseas and pay their workers a few pennies a day too. This contributes to a recession. Americans lose their jobs, stop paying taxes, and start collecting government benefits like Medicaid and unemployment. This means that Uncle Sam has even less income and even more expenses. At the same time, the people who still have jobs are desperate to keep them, so they tend to do more work but not to get paid any more. When your dollars are worth less, and you're not earning more of them, that's called stagflation. And this is why Uncle Sam is in a Catch 22. He can't raise taxes or cut spending without making the recession worse. And he can't have the Federal Reserve create more money without making inflation worse. For now, he can keep borrowing more money but since he can't even pay the interest on the loans he already has, it just makes his inevitable bankruptcy even worse. Whether it's in two months or two years, the day will come when Uncle Sam can no longer pay his bills. When that happens, investors, and foreign governments who are counting on that money won't be able to pay their bill. You see, just like Uncle Sam, governments, banks, and corporations don't actually have much money. Mostly, all they have is debt to each other. If one link in a debt chain stops paying, defaults, the whole thing falls apart. If investors can't pay their bills, corporations won't be able to pay their employees. If banks can't pay their bills, you won't be able to take out loan, use a credit card or even withdraw your savings. If foreign governments can't pay their bills, their own banks and corporations will have the same problems. That's called a global economic collapse. It's never happened before, so nobody really knows how bad it will be, how long it will last, or even how we'll eventually get out of it. The house of cards has already been built. There's no painless way to dismantle it now. All we can do is to educate each other about what's actually going on and to prepare for what may be very extraordinary circumstances.

- *Video Appreciation: How Pig Parts Make the World Turn*

Hello. I would like to start my talk with actually two questions, and the first one is: How many people here actually eat pig meat? Please raise your hand — oh, that's a lot. And how many people have actually seen a live pig producing this meat? In the last year?

In the Netherlands — where I come from — you actually never see a pig, which is really strange, because, on a population of 16 million people, we have 12 million pigs. And well, of course, the Dutch can't eat all these pigs. They eat about one-third, and the rest is exported to all kinds of countries in Europe and the rest of the world. A lot goes to the U.K., Germany.

And what I was curious about — because historically, the whole pig would be used up until the last bit so nothing would be wasted — and I was curious to find out if this was actually still the case. And I spent about three years researching. And I followed this one pig with number "05049," all the way up until the end and to what products it's made of. And in these years, I met all kinds people like, for instance, farmers and butchers, which seems logical. But I also met aluminum mold makers, ammunition producers and all kinds of people. And what was striking to me is that the farmers actually had no clue what was made of their pigs, but the consumers — as in us — had also no idea of the pigs being in all these products.

So what I did is, I took all this research and I made it into a — well, basically it's a product catalog of this one pig, and it carries a duplicate of his ear tag on the back. And it consists of seven chapters—the chapters are skin, bones, meat, internal organs, blood, fat and miscellaneous. (Laughter) In total, they weigh 103.7 kilograms. And to show you how often you actually meet part of this pig in a regular day, I want to show you some images of the book.

You probably start the day with a shower. So, in soap, fatty acids made from boiling pork bone fat are used as a hardening agent, but also for giving it a pearl-like effect. Then if you look around you in the bathroom, you see lots more products like shampoo, conditioner, anti-wrinkle cream, body lotion, but also toothpaste. Then, so, before breakfast, you've already met the pig so many times. Then, at breakfast, the pig that I followed, the hairs off the pig or proteins from the hairs off the pig were used as an improver of dough. (Laughter) Well, that's what the producer says: it's "improving the dough, of course." In low-fat butter or actually in many low-fat products, when you take the fat out, you actually take the taste and the texture out. So what they do is they put gelatin back in, in order to retain the texture.

Well, when you're off to work, under the road or under the buildings that you see, there might very well be cellular concrete, which is a very light kind of concrete that's actually got proteins from bones inside and it's also fully reusable. In the train brakes — at least in the German train brakes — there's this part of the brake that's made of bone ash. And in cheesecake and all kinds of desserts, like chocolate mousse, tiramisu, vanilla pudding, everything that's cooled in the supermarket, there's gelatin to make it look good. Fine bone china — this is a real classic. Of course, the bone in fine-bone china gives it its translucency and also its strength, in order to make these really fine shapes, like this deer.

In interior decorating, the pig's actually quite there. It's used in paint for the texture, but also for the glossiness. In sandpaper, bone glue is actually the glue between the sand and the paper. And then in paintbrushes, hairs are used because, apparently, they're very suitable for making paintbrushes because of their hard-wearing nature.

You probably all know what meats they are. But I didn't want you to miss out on this one, because this, well, it's called "portion-controlled meat cuts." And this is actually sold in the frozen area of the supermarket. And what it is — it's actually steak. So, this is sold as cow, but what happens when you slaughter a cow — at least in industrial factory farming — they have all these little bits of steak left that they can't actually sell as steak, so what they do is they glue them all together with fibrin from pig blood into this really large sausage, then freeze the sausage, cut it in little slices and sell those as steak again. And this also actually happens with tuna and scallops. So, with the steak, you might drink a beer. In the brewing process, there are lots of cloudy elements in the beer, so to get rid of these cloudy elements, what some companies do is they pour the beer through a sort of gelatin sieve in order to get rid of that cloudiness. This actually also goes for wine as well as fruit juice.

There's actually a company in Greece that produces these cigarettes that actually contain hemoglobin from pigs in the filter. And according to them, this creates an artificial lung in the filter. (Laughter) So, this is actually a healthier cigarette. (Laughter) Injectable collagen—or, since the '70s, collagen from pigs—has been used for injecting into wrinkles. And the reason for this is that pigs are actually quite close to human beings, so the collagen is as well. Well, this must be the strangest thing I found. This is a bullet coming from a very large ammunition company in the United States.

And while I was making the book, I contacted all the producers of products because I wanted them to send me the real samples and the real specimens. So I sent this company an email saying, "Hello. I'm Christien. I'm doing this research. And can you send me a bullet?" (Laughter) And well, I didn't expect them to even answer my email. But they answered and they said, "Why, thank you for your email. What an interesting story. Are you in anyway related to the Dutch government?" I thought that was really weird, as if the Dutch government sends emails to anyone. (Laughter)

So, the most beautiful thing I found — at least what I think is the most beautiful — in the book, is this heart valve. It's actually a very low-tech and very high-tech product at the same time. The low-tech bit is that it's literally a pig's heart valve mounted in the high-tech bit, which is a memory metal casing. And what happens is this can be implanted into a human heart without open heart surgery. And once it's in the right spot, they remove the outer shell, and the heart valve, well, it gets this shape and at that moment it starts beating, instantly. It's really a sort of magical moment. So this is actually a Dutch company, so I called them up, and I asked, "Can I borrow a heart valve from you?" And the makers of this thing were really enthusiastic. So they were like, "Okay, we'll put it in a jar for you with formalin, and you can borrow it." Great — and then I didn't hear from them for weeks, so I called, and I asked, "What's going on with the heart valve?" And they said, "Well the director of the company decided not to let you borrow this heart valve, because he doesn't want his product to be associated with pigs." (Laughter)

Well, the last product from the book that I'm showing you is renewable energy — actually, to show that my first question, if pigs are still used up until the last bit, was still true. Well it is, because everything that can't be used for anything else is made into a fuel that can be used as renewable energy source.

In total, I found 185 products. And what they showed me is that, well, firstly, it's at least to say odd that we don't treat these pigs as absolute kings and queens. And the second, is that we actually don't have a clue of what all these products that surround us are made of.

And you might think I'm very fond of pigs, but actually — well, I am a little bit—but I'm more fond of raw materials in general. And I think that, in order to take better care of what's behind our products — so, the livestock, the crops, the plants, the non-renewable materials, but also the people that produce these products—the first step would actually be to know that they are there.

Thank you very much. (Applause)

◇ **Section A**

• **Conversation One**

M: So how long have you been a Market Research Consultant?

W: Well, I started straight after finishing university.

M: Did you study market research?

W: Yeah, and it really helped me to get into the industry, but I have to say that it's more important to get experience in different types of market research to find out exactly what you're interested in.

M: So what are you interested in?

W: Well, at the moment, I specialize in quantitative advertising research, which means that I do two types of projects. Trackers, which are ongoing projects that look at trends or customer satisfaction over a long period of time. The only problem with trackers is that it takes up a lot of your time. But you do build up a good relationship with the client. I also do a couple of ad-hoc jobs which are much shorter projects.

M: What exactly do you mean by ad-hoc jobs?

W: It's basically when companies need quick answers to their questions about their consumers' habits. They just ask for one questionnaire to be sent out for example, so the time you spend on an ad-hoc project tends to be fairly short.

M: Which do you prefer, trackers or ad-hoc?

W: I like doing both and in fact I need to do both at the same time to keep me from going crazy. I need the variety.

M: Can you just explain what process you go through with a new client?

W: Well, together we decide on the methodology and the objectives of the research. I then design a questionnaire. Once the interviewers have been briefed, I send the client a schedule and then they get back to me with deadlines. Once the final charts and tables are ready, I have to check them and organize a presentation.

M: Hmm, one last question, what do you like and dislike about your job?

W: As I said, variety is important and as for what I don't like, it has to be the checking of charts and tables.

Questions 1 to 4 are based on the conversation you have just heard.

1. What position does the woman hold in the company?

2. What does the woman specialize in at the moment?

3. What does the woman say about trackers?

4. What does the woman dislike about her job?

• **Conversation Two**

W: Hello, I'm here with Frederick. Now Fred, you went to university in Canada?

M: Yeah, that's right.

W: OK, and you have very strong views about universities in Canada. Could you please explain?

M: Well, we don't have private universities in Canada. They're all public. All the universities are owned by the government, so there is the Ministry of Education in charge of creating the curriculum for the universities and so there is not much room for flexibility. Since it's a government-operated institution, things don't move very fast. If you want something to be done, then their staff do not have so much incentive to help you because he's a worker for the government. So I don't think it's very efficient. However, there are certain advantages of public universities, such as the fees being free. You don't have to pay for your education. But the system isn't efficient, and it does not work that well.

W: Yeah, I can see your point, but in the United States we have many private universities, and I think they are large bureaucracies also. Maybe people don't act that much differently, because it's the same thing working for a private university. They get paid for their job. I don't know if they're that much more motivated to help people. Also, we have a problem in the United States that usually only wealthy kids go to the best schools and it's kind of a   problem actually.

M: I agree with you. I think it's a problem because you're not giving equal access to education to everybody. It's not easy, but having only public universities also might not be the best solution. Perhaps we can learn from Japan where they have a system of private and public universities. Now, in Japan, public universities are considered to be the best.

W: Right. It's the exact opposite in the United States.

M: So, as you see，it's very hard to say which one is better.

W: Right, a good point.

Questions 5 to 8 are based on the conversation you have just heard.

5. What does the woman want Frederick to talk about?

6. What does the man say about the curriculum in Canadian universities?

7. On what point do the speakers agree?

8. What point does the man make at the end of the conversation?

◇ Section B

· **Passage One**

A recent International Labor Organization report says the deterioration of real wages around the world calls into question the true extent of an economic recovery, especially if government rescue packages are phased out too early. The report warns the picture on wages is likely to get worse this year despite indications of an economic rebound. Patrick Belser, an international labor organization specialist, says declining wage rates are linked to the levels of unemployment. The quite dramatic unemployment features, which we now see in some of the countries, strongly suggest that there will be a great pressure on wages in the future as more people will be unemployed, more people will be looking for jobs and the pressure on employers to raise wages to attract workers will decline. So we expect that the second part of the year would not be very good in terms of wage growth. The report finds more than a quarter of the countries experienced flat or falling monthly wages in real terms. They include the United States, Austria, Costa Rica, South Africa and Germany. International Labor Organization economists say some nations have come up with policies to lessen the impact of lower wages during the economic crisis. An example of these is work sharing with government subsidies. Under this scheme, the number of individual working hours is reduced in an effort to avoid layoffs. For this scheme to work, the government must provide wage subsidies to compensate for lost pay due to the shorter hours.

Questions 9 to 11 are based on the passage you have just heard.

9. What is the International Labor Organization's report mainly about?

10. According to an International Labor Organization's specialist, how will employers feel if there are more people looking for jobs?

11. What does the speaker mean by the work sharing scheme?

· Passage Two

Is there really a magic memory pill or a herbal recall remedy? I have been frequently asked if these memory supplements work. You know, one of the first things I like to tell people when they ask me about the supplements, is that a lot of them are promoted as a cure for your memory. But your memory doesn't need a cure. What your memory needs is a good workout. So really those supplements aren't going to give you that perfect memory in the way that they promise. The other thing is that a lot of these supplements aren't necessarily what they claim to be, and you really have to be wary when you take any of them. The science isn't there behind most of them. They're not really well-regulated unless they adhere to some industry standard. You don't really know that what they say is in there, isn't there. What you must understand is that those supplements especially in some eastern cultures, are part of a medical practice tradition. People don't just go, in a local grocery store and buy these supplements. In fact, they are prescribed and they're given at a certain level, a dosage that is understood by a practitioner who's been trained. And that's not really the way they're used in this country. The other tiling people do forget is that these are medicines, so they do have an impact. A lot of times people are not really aware of the impact they have, or the fact that taking them in combination with other medications might put you at increased risk for something that you wouldn't otherwise being countering or be at risk for.

Questions 12 to 15 are based on the passage you have just heard.

12. What question is frequently put to the speaker?

13. What does the speaker say about most memory supplements?

14. What do we learn about memory supplements in eastern cultures?

15. What does the speaker say about memory supplements at the end?

◈ Section C

· Recording One

The negative impacts of natural disasters can be seen everywhere. In just the past few weeks, the world has witnessed the destructive powers of earthquakes in Indonesia, typhoons in the Philippines, and the destructive sea waves that struck Samoa and neighboring islands. A study by the Center for Research on the Epidemiology of Disasters finds that, between 1980 and 2007, nearly 8,400 natural disasters killed more than two million people. These catastrophic events caused more than $1.5 trillion in economic losses.

U.N. weather expert Geoffrey Love says that is the bad news. "Over the last 50 years, economic losses have increased by a factor of 50. That sounds pretty terrible, but the loss of life has decreased by a factor of 10 simply because we are getting better at warning people. We are making a difference. Extreme events, however, will continue to occur. But, the message is that they need not be disasters."

Love, who is director of Weather and Disaster Risk Reduction at the World Meteorological Organization, says most of the deaths and economic losses were caused by weather, climate, or water-related extremes. These include droughts, floods, windstorms, strong tropical winds and wildfires. He says extreme events will continue. But, he says extreme events become disasters only when people fail to prepare for them.

"Many of the remedies are well-known. From a planning perspective, it is pretty simple. Build better buildings. Don't build where the hazards will destroy them. From an early-warning perspective, make sure the warnings go right down to the community level. Build community action plans."

The World Meteorological Organization points to Cuba and Bangladesh as examples of countries that have successfully reduced the loss of life caused by natural disasters by taking preventive action.

It says tropical storms formerly claimed dozens, if not hundreds of lives, each year, in Cuba. But, the development of an early-warning system has reversed that trend. In 2008, Cuba was hit by five successive hurricanes, but only seven people were killed.

Bangladesh also has achieved substantial results. Major storm surges in 1970 and 1991 caused the deaths of about 440,000 people. Through careful preparation，the death toll from a super tropical storm in November 2007 was less than 3,500.

Questions 16 to 18 are based on the recording you have just heard.

16. What is the talk mainly about?

17. How can we stop extreme events from turning into disasters?

18. What does the example of Cuba serve to show?

- **Recording Two**

As U.S. banks recovered with the help of the American government and the American taxpayer, President Obama held meetings with top bank executives, telling them it's time to return the favor. "The way I see it are banks now having a greater obligation to the goal of a wider recovery," he said. But the president may be giving the financial sector too much credit, "It was in a free fall，and it was a very scary period." Economist Martin Neil Baily said. After the failure of Lehman Brothers, many of the world's largest banks feared the worst as the collapse of the housing bubble exposed in investments in risky loans.

Although he says the worst is just over, Baily says the banking crisis is not. More than 130 US banks failed in 2009. He predicts high failure rates for smaller, regional banks in 2010 as commercial real estate loans come due. "So there may actually be a worsening of credit availability to small and medium sized businesses in the next year or so."

Analysts say the biggest problem is high unemployment, which weakens demand and makes banks reluctant to lend. But US Bankcorp chief Richard Davis sees the situation differently. "We're probably more optimistic than the experts might be. With that in mind, we're putting in everything we can, lending is the coal to our engine, so we want to make more loans. We have to find a way to qualify more people and not put ourselves at risk."

While some economists predict continued recovery in the future, Baily says the only certainty is that banks are unlikely to make the same mistakes twice. "You know, forecasting's become a very hazardous business so I don't want to commit myself too much. I don't think we know exactly what's going to happen but it's certainly possible that we could get very slow growth over the next year or two."

If the economy starts to shrink again, Baily says it would make a strong case for a second stimulus—something the Obama administration hopes will not be necessary.

Questions 19 to 22 are based on the recording you have just heard.

19. What does President Obama hope the banks will do?

20. What is Martin Neil Baily's prediction about the financial situation in the future?

21. What does U.S. Bankcorp chief Richard Davis say about its future operation?

22. What does Martin Neil Baily think of a second stimulus to the economy?

- **Recording Three**

A new study has failed to find any conclusive evidence that lifestyle changes can prevent cognitive decline in older adults. Still there are good reasons to make positive changes in how we live and what we eat as we age. Cognitive decline is the loss of ability to learn new skills, or recall words, names, and faces that is most common as we age. To reduce or avoid it, researchers have examined the effect of smoking, diet, brain-challenging games, exercise and other strategies.

Researchers at Duke University scrutinized more than 160 published studies and found an absence of strong evidence that any of these approaches can make a big difference. Co-author James Burke helped design the study. "In the observational studies we found that some of the B vitamins were beneficial." "Exercise, diet, cognitive stimulation showed some positive effects, although the evidence was not so strong that we could actually consider these firmly established." Some previous studies have suggested that challenging your brain with mentally stimulating activities might help. And Burke says that actually does seem to help, based on randomized studies—the researcher's gold standard "Cognitive stimulation is one of the areas where we did find some benefit. The exact type of stimulation that an individual uses is not as important as being intellectually engaged." The expert review also found insufficient evidence to recommend any drugs or dietary supplements that could prevent or slow cognitive decline. However, given that there is at least some evidence for positive effects from some of these lifestyle changes, plus other benefits apparently unrelated to cognitive decline, Burke was willing to offer some recommendations. "I think that by having people adopt a healthy lifestyle, both from a medical standpoint as well as nutritional and cognitive stimulation standpoint, we can reduce the incidence of cognitive decline, which will be proof that these factors are, in fact, important." James Burke of Duke University is one of the authors of a study reviewing previous research on cognitive decline. The paper is published online by the Annals of Internal Medicine.

Questions 23 to 25 are based on the recording you have just heard.

23. According to the speaker, what might be a symptom of cognitive decline in older adults?

24. According to James Burke, what does seem to help reduce cognitive decline?

25. What did James Burke recommend to reduce the incidence of cognitive decline?

■ Chapter 5

• **Compound Dictation One**

Art Expands Horizons

As a conceptual artist, I'm constantly looking for creative ways to spark challenging conversations. I do this through painting, sculpture, video and performance. But regardless of the format, two of my favorite materials are history and dialogue.

In 2007, I created "Lotus," a seven-and-a-half-foot diameter, 600-pound glass depiction of a lotus blossom. In Buddhism, the lotus is a symbol for transcendence and for purity of mind and spirit. But a closer look at this lotus reveals each petal to be the cross-section of a slave ship. This iconic diagram was taken from a British slaving manual and later used by abolitionists to show the atrocities of slavery. In America, we don't like to talk about slavery, nor do we look at it as a global industry. But by using this Buddhist symbol, I hope to universalize and transcend the history and trauma of black America and encourage discussions about our shared past.

To create "Lotus," we carved over 6,000 figures. And this later led to a commission by the City of New York to create a 28-foot version in steel as a permanent installation at the Eagle Academy for Young Men, a school for black and Latino students, the two groups most affected by this history. The same two groups are very affected by a more recent phenomenon, but let me digress.

I've been collecting wooden African figures from tourist shops and flea markets around the world. The authenticity and origin of them is completely debatable, but people believe these to be imbued with power, or even magic. Only recently have I figured out how to use this in my own work.

(Gun shots)

Since 2012, the world has witnessed the killings of Trayvon Martin, Michael Brown, Eric Garner, Sandra Bland, Tamir Rice and literally countless other unarmed black citizens at the hands of the police, who frequently walk away with no punishment at all. In consideration of these victims and the several times that even I, a law-abiding, Ivy League professor, have been targeted and harassed at gunpoint by the police. I created this body of work simply entitled "BAM."

It was important to erase the identity of each of these figures, to make them all look the same and easier to disregard. To do this, I dip them in a thick, brown wax before taking them to a shooting range where I re-sculpted them using bullets. And it was fun, playing with big guns and high-speed video cameras. But my reverence for these figures kept me from actually pulling the trigger, somehow feeling as if I would be shooting myself. Finally, my cameraman, Raul, fired the shots. I then took the fragments of these and created molds, and cast them first in wax, and finally in bronze like the image you see here, which bears the marks of its violent creation like battle wounds or scars.

When I showed this work recently in Miami, a woman told me she felt every gun shot to her soul. But she also felt that these artworks memorialized the victims of these killings as well as other victims of racial violence throughout US history.

But "Lotus" and "BAM" are larger than just US history. While showing in Berlin last year, a philosophy student asked me what prompted these recent killings. I showed him a photo of a lynching postcard from the early 1900s and reminded him that these killings have been going on for over 500 years. But it's only through questions like his and more thoughtful dialogue about history and race can we evolve as individuals and society.

I hope my artwork creates a safe space for this type of honest exchange and an opportunity for people to engage one another in real and necessary conversation.

Thank you. (Applause)

- **Compound Dictation Two**

Three Ways to Fix a Broken News Industry

Five years ago, I had my dream job. I was a foreign correspondent in the Middle East reporting for ABC News. But there was a crack in the wall, a problem with our industry that I felt we needed to fix. You see, I got to the Middle East right around the end of 2007, which was just around the midpoint of the Iraq War. But by the time I got there, it was already nearly impossible to find stories about Iraq on air. Coverage had dropped across the board, across networks. And of the stories that did make it, more than 80 percent of them were about us. We were missing the stories about Iraq, the people who live there, and what was happening to them under the weight of the war.

Afghanistan had already fallen off the agenda. There were less than one percent of all news stories in 2008 that went to the war in Afghanistan. It was the longest war in US history, but information was so scarce that school teachers we spoke to told us they had trouble explaining to their students what we were doing there, when those students had parents who were fighting and sometimes dying overseas.

We had drawn a blank, and it wasn't just Iraq and Afghanistan. From conflict zones to climate change to all sorts of issues around crises in public health, we were missing what I call the species-level issues, because as a species, they could actually sink us. And by failing to understand the complex issues of our time, we were facing certain practical implications. How were we going to solve problems that we didn't fundamentally understand, that we couldn't track in real time, and where the people working on the issues were invisible to us and sometimes invisible to each other?

When you look back on Iraq, those years when we were missing the story, were the years when the society was falling apart, when we were setting the conditions for what would become the rise of ISIS, the ISIS takeover of Mosul and terrorist violence that would spread beyond Iraq's borders to the rest of the world.

Just around that time where I was making that observation, I looked across the border of Iraq and noticed there was another story we were missing: the war in Syria. If you were a Middle-East specialist, you knew that Syria was that important from the start. But it ended up being, really, one of the forgotten stories of the Arab Spring. I saw the implications up front. Syria is intimately tied to regional security, to global stability. I felt like we couldn't let that become another one of the stories we left behind.

So I left my big TV job to start a website, called "Syria Deeply." It was designed to be a news and information source that made it easier to understand a complex issue, and for the past four years, it's been a resource for policymakers and professionals working on the conflict in Syria. We built a business model based on consistent, high-quality information, and convening the top minds on the issue. And we found it was a model that scaled. We got passionate requests to do other things "Deeply." So we started to work our way down the list.

I'm just one of many entrepreneurs, and we are just one of many start-ups trying to fix what's wrong with news. All of us in the trenches know that something is wrong with the news industry. It's broken. Trust in the media has hit an all-time low. And the statistic you're seeing up there is from September — it's arguably gotten worse. But we can fix this. We can fix the news. I know that that's true. You can call me an idealist; I call myself an industrious optimist. And I know there are a lot of us out there. We have ideas for how to make things better, and I want to share three of them that we've picked up in our own work.

Idea number one: we need news that's built on deep-domain knowledge. Given the waves and waves of layoffs at newsrooms across the country, we've lost the art of specialization. Beat reporting is an endangered thing. When it comes to foreign news, the way we can fix that is by working with more local journalists, treating them like our partners and collaborators, not just fixers who fetch us phone numbers and sound bites. Our local reporters in Syria and across Africa and across Asia bring us stories that we certainly would not have found on our own. Like this one from the suburbs of Damascus, about a wheelchair race that gave hope to those wounded in the war. Or this one from Sierra Leone, about a local chief who curbed the spread of Ebola by self-organizing a quarantine in his district. Or this one from the border of Pakistan, about Afghan refugees being forced to return home before they are ready, under the threat of police intimidation. Our local journalists are our mentors. They teach us something new every day, and they bring us stories that are important for all of us to know.

Idea number two: we need a kind of Hippocratic oath for the news industry, a pledge to first do no harm. Journalists need to be tough. We need to speak truth to power, but we also need to be responsible. We need to live up to our own ideals, and we need to recognize when what we're doing could potentially harm society, where we lose track of journalism as a public service.

I watched us cover the Ebola crisis. We launched Ebola Deeply. We did our best. But what we saw was a public that was flooded with hysterical and sensational coverage, sometimes inaccurate, sometimes completely wrong. Public health experts tell me that actually cost us in human lives, because by sparking more panic and by sometimes getting the facts wrong, we made it harder for people to resolve what was actually happening on the ground. All that noise made it harder to make the right decisions.

We can do better as an industry, but it requires us recognizing how we got it wrong last time, and deciding not to go that way next time. It's a choice. We have to resist the temptation to use fear for ratings. And that decision has to be made in the individual newsroom and with the individual news executive. Because the next deadly virus that comes around could be much worse and the consequences much higher, if we do what we did last time; if our reporting isn't responsible and it isn't right.

The third idea? We need to embrace complexity if we want to make sense of a complex world. Embrace complexity — not treat the world simplistically, because simple isn't accurate. We live in a complex world. News is adult education. It's our job as journalists to get elbow deep in complexity and to find new ways to make it easier for everyone else to understand. If we don't do that, if we pretend there are just simple answers, we're leading everyone off a steep cliff. Understanding complexity is the only way to know the real threats that are around the corner. It's our responsibility to translate those threats and to help you understand what's real, so you can be prepared and know what it takes to be ready for what comes next.

I am an industrious optimist. I do believe we can fix what's broken. We all want to. There are great journalists out there doing great work—we just need new formats. I honestly believe this is a time of reawakening, reimagining what we can do. I believe we can fix what's broken. I know we can fix the news. I know it's worth trying, and I truly believe that in the end, we're going to get this right. Thank you.

- ### *Video Appreciation: Body Language*

So I want to start by offering you a free no-tech life hack, and all it requires of you is this: that you change your posture for two minutes. But before I give it away, I want to ask you to right now do a little audit of your body and what you're doing with your body. So how many of you are sort of making yourselves smaller? Maybe you're hunching, crossing your legs, maybe wrapping your ankles. Sometimes we hold onto our arms like this. Sometimes we spread out. (Laughter) I see you. So I want you to pay attention to what you're doing right now. We're going to come back to that in a few minutes, and I'm hoping that if you learn to tweak this a little bit, it could significantly change the way your life unfolds.

So, we're really fascinated with body language, and we're particularly interested in other people's body language. You know, we're interested in, like, you know — (Laughter) — an awkward interaction, or a smile, or a contemptuous glance, or maybe a very awkward wink, or maybe even something like a handshake.

Narrator: Here they are arriving at Number 10. This lucky policeman gets to shake hands with the President of the United States. Here comes the Prime Minister — No. Amy Cuddy: So a handshake, or the lack of a handshake, can have us talking for weeks and weeks and weeks. Even the BBC and The New York Times. So obviously when we think about nonverbal behavior, or body language — but we call it nonverbals as social scientists — it's language, so we think about communication. When we think about communication, we think about interactions. So what is your body language communicating to me? What's mine communicating to you?

And there's a lot of reason to believe that this is a valid way to look at this. So social scientists have spent a lot of time looking at the effects of our body language, or other people's body language, on judgments. And we make sweeping judgments and inferences from body language. And those judgments can predict really meaningful life outcomes like who we hire or promote, who we ask out on a date. For example, Nalini Ambady, a researcher at Tufts University, shows that when people watch 30-second soundless clips of real physician-patient interactions, their judgments of the physician's niceness predict whether or not that physician will be sued. So it doesn't have to do so much with whether or not that physician was incompetent, but do we like that person and how they interacted? Even more dramatic, Alex Todorov at Princeton has shown us that judgments of political candidates' faces in just one second predict 70 percent of U.S. Senate and gubernatorial race outcomes, and even, let's go digital, emoticons used well in online negotiations can lead you to claim more value from that negotiation. If you use them poorly, bad idea. Right?

So when we think of nonverbals, we think of how we judge others, how they judge us and what the outcomes are. We tend to forget, though, the other audience that's influenced by our nonverbals, and that's ourselves. We are also influenced by our nonverbals, our thoughts and our feelings and our physiology.

So what nonverbals am I talking about? I'm a social psychologist. I study prejudice, and I teach at a competitive business school, so it was inevitable that I would become interested in power dynamics. I became especially interested in nonverbal expressions of power and dominance.

And what are nonverbal expressions of power and dominance? Well, this is what they are. So in the animal kingdom, they are about expanding. So you make yourself big, you stretch out, you take up space, you're basically opening up. It's about opening up. And this is true across the animal kingdom. It's not just limited to primates. And humans do the same thing. (Laughter) So they do this both when they have power sort of chronically, and also when they're feeling powerful in the moment. And this one is especially interesting because it really shows us how universal and old these expressions of power are. This expression, which is known as pride, Jessica Tracy has studied. She shows that people who are born with sight and people who are congenitally blind do this when they win at a physical competition. So when they cross the finish line and they've won, it doesn't matter if they've never seen anyone do it. They do this. So the arms up in the V, the chin is slightly lifted.

What do we do when we feel powerless? We do exactly the opposite. We close up. We wrap ourselves up. We make ourselves small. We don't want to bump into the person next to us. So again, both animals and humans do the same thing. And this is what happens when you put together high and low power. So what we tend to do when it comes to power is that we complement the other's nonverbals. So if someone is being really powerful with us, we tend to make ourselves smaller. We don't mirror them. We do the opposite of them.

So I'm watching this behavior in the classroom, and what do I notice? I notice that MBA students really exhibit the full range of power nonverbals. So you have people who are like caricatures of alphas, really coming into the room, they get right into the middle of the room before class even starts, like they really want to occupy space. When they sit down, they're sort of spread out. They raise their hands like this. You have other people who are virtually collapsing when they come in. As soon they come in, you see it. You see it on their faces and their bodies, and they sit in their chair and they make themselves tiny, and they go like this when they raise their hand.

I notice a couple of things about this. One, you're not going to be surprised. It seems to be related to gender. So women are much more likely to do this kind of thing than men. Women feel chronically less powerful than men, so this is not surprising.

But the other thing I noticed is that it also seemed to be related to the extent to which the students were participating, and how well they were participating. And this is really important in the MBA classroom, because participation counts for half the grade.

So business schools have been struggling with this gender grade gap. You get these equally qualified women and men coming in and then you get these differences in grades, and it seems to be partly attributable to participation. So I started to wonder, you know, okay, so you have these people coming in like this, and they're participating. Is it possible that we could get people to fake it and would it lead them to participate more?

So my main collaborator Dana Carney, who's at Berkeley, and I really wanted to know, can you fake it till you make it? Like, can you do this just for a little while and actually experience a behavioral outcome that makes you seem more powerful? So we know that our nonverbals govern how other people think and feel about us. There's a lot of evidence. But our question really was, do our nonverbals govern how we think and feel about ourselves?

There's some evidence that they do. So, for example, we smile when we feel happy, but also, when we're forced to smile by holding a pen in our teeth like this, it makes us feel happy. So it goes both ways. When it comes to power, it also goes both ways. So when you feel powerful, you're more likely to do this, but it's also possible that when you pretend to be powerful, you are more likely to actually feel powerful.

So the second question really was, you know, so we know that our minds change our bodies, but is it also true that our bodies change our minds? And when I say minds, in the case of the powerful, what am I talking about? So I'm talking about thoughts and feelings and the sort of physiological things that make up our thoughts and feelings, and in my case, that's hormones. I look at hormones. So what do the minds of the powerful versus the powerless look like? So powerful people tend to be, not surprisingly, more assertive and more confident, more optimistic. They actually feel they're going to win even at games of chance. They also tend to be able to think more abstractly. So there are a lot of differences. They take more risks. There are a lot of differences between powerful and powerless people. Physiologically, there also are differences on two key hormones: testosterone, which is the dominance hormone, and cortisol, which is the stress hormone.

So what we find is that high-power alpha males in primate hierarchies have high testosterone and low cortisol, and powerful and effective leaders also have high testosterone and low cortisol. So what does that mean? When you think about power, people tended to think only about testosterone, because that was about dominance. But really, power is also about how you react to stress. So do you want the high-power leader that's dominant, high on testosterone, but really stress reactive? Probably not, right? You want the person who's powerful and assertive and dominant, but not very stress reactive, the person who's laid back.

So we know that in primate hierarchies, if an alpha needs to take over, if an individual needs to take over an alpha role sort of suddenly, within a few days, that individual's testosterone has gone up significantly and his cortisol has dropped significantly. So we have this evidence, both that the body can shape the mind, at least at the facial level, and also that role changes can shape the mind. So what happens, okay, you take a role change, what happens if you do that at a really minimal level, like this tiny manipulation, this tiny intervention? "For two minutes," you say, "I want you to stand like this, and it's going to make you feel more powerful."

So this is what we did. We decided to bring people into the lab and run a little experiment, and these people adopted, for two minutes, either high-power poses or low-power poses, and I'm just going to show you five of the poses, although they took on only two. So here's one. A couple more. This one has been dubbed the "Wonder Woman" by the media. Here are a couple more. So you can be standing or you can be sitting. And here are the low-power poses. So you're folding up, you're making yourself small. This one is very low-power. When you're touching your neck, you're really protecting yourself.

So this is what happens. They come in, they spit into a vial, for two minutes, we say, "You need to do this or this." They don't look at pictures of the poses. We don't want to prime them with a concept of power. We want them to be feeling power. So two minutes they do this. We then ask them, "How powerful do you feel?" on a series of items, and then we give them an opportunity to gamble, and then we take another saliva sample. That's it. That's the whole experiment.

So this is what we find. Risk tolerance, which is the gambling, we find that when you are in the high-power pose condition, 86 percent of you will gamble. When you're in the low-power pose condition, only 60 percent, and that's a whopping significant difference. Here's what we find on testosterone. From their baseline when they come in, high-power people experience about a 20-percent increase, and low-power people experience about a 10-percent decrease. So again, two minutes, and you get these changes.

◇ **Section A**

· **Conversation One**

W: Art Department, the treasurer Brown speaking.

M: Hello, Professor Brown, my name is Frank Meloy. I'm thinking of taking your course in spray painting, and I'm calling to find more about it.

W: Have you ever worked with spray paints?

M: I've done very little painting at all. I'm a chemistry major, but I enjoy drawing and the course description says that any student can sign up. I assume that means that experience in painting isn't necessary.

W: Yes, that's right. We'll be using spray paints instead of oils because they are easier to handle and dry more quickly. Also, beginning students can get a good feeling for what they can do with textures by working with spray paints.

M: My roommate is also a chemistry major but he has painted quite a bit. If he signed up for the course, would he find it too easy?

W: No, he could work on using techniques he already knows and applying them to principles of composition, color and design. There's something for everyone in this course.

M: One more question: Do we need to bring our own brushes and paints to class?

W: Yes, you can buy them at the bookstore. I'll provide drawing board and any other supplies that are necessary. I hope you decide to join us.

M: It sounds interesting. I'll definitely register today. I know it's the deadline.

W: Fine. See you next Monday afternoon. Don't forget your brushes and paints.

M: Thank you very much, professor.

W: You're welcome.

Questions 1 to 4 are based on the conversation you have just heard.

1. What is the man calling about?

2. According to the woman, what is one main advantage of the spray paints?

3. What might the man's roommate do if he joins in?

4. What will the man do before the end of the day?

• **Conversation Two**

W: Hi, Tom.

M: Judy! I haven't seen you in weeks. Where have you been?

W: In Florida.

M: What? Vacationing while the rest of us have been studying on campus in the February cold?

W: Not exactly. I spent most of my time underwater.

M: I don't understand.

W: I was on a special field trip. I went with my marine biology class.

M: So you went scuba diving. What were you looking for, sunken treasure?

W: You might say so. The sea is full of treasures, all kinds of strange fascinating organisms. Our class concentrated on studying plankton.

M: I thought plankton are too small to be seen.

W: That's a common misconception. As a matter of fact, the term Plankton covers a wide variety of freely floating plants and animals from microscopic one-celled organism to large ones such as the common jellyfish.

M: Jellyfish may be large enough to be seen, but they are transparent, aren't they?

W: Yes, most plankton have transparent tissues as a way of protection. It makes them practically invisible to predators.

M: But not invisible to your biology class, I hope.

W: By concentrating, I was able to see the outlines of lots of different plankton. In fact, our professor even took photographs of Greeber Quadata, which are small oceanic snails.

M: That sounds like an interesting trip. But I think if I'd been in Florida in February, I'd much rather spend my time just swimming and lying in the sun.

W: I bet you would.

Questions 5 to 8 are based on the conversation you have just heard.

5. How did Judy spend most of her time in Florida?

6. What was Tom doing in February?

7. What do we learn about the plankton?

8. Why is it hard to see most plankton?

◇ Section B

· Passage One

French wine-making began more than 2,500 years ago. The world's oldest type of vine grows in France and always produces a good quality wine. Today France produces one-fifth of the world's wine, and some of the most famous varieties. The top wine-producing areas are Bordeaux, Burgundy and the Loire Valley. Champagne, a drink used in celebrations, is named after the place where sparkling wine was first produced in 1700. Wine is made from the juice of freshly picked grapes. It is the sugars that turn into alcohol. Traditionally, people used to take off their shoes and crush the grapes with their bare feet to bring out the juice. Nowadays, this practice is usually carried out by machines. Each wine-producing region has its own character, based on its type of grapes and soil. The taste of wine changes with time. Until 1850, all French champagne was sweet. Now, both wine and champagne taste slightly bitter. The drink has always been linked with riches, romance and nobleness. Yet the French think of it in more ordinary terms. They believe it makes daily living easier, less hurried and with fewer problems. Wine drinking has become part of the French lifestyle, just like tea has for the Chinese. For a Frenchman, it is possible to start drinking wine at breakfast, carry on until the early hours of the next morning, and still be able to walk in a straight line.

Questions 9 to 12 are based on the passage you have just heard.

9. How was the name "Champagne" given?

10. How was the juice of grapes brought out in the past?

11. How has French champagne changed over more than a century?

12. What does "wine" mean to French people?

· Passage Two

The Chinese Antarctica expedition returned to Shanghai on March 20 following a month living on the ice. It was the first time Chinese scientists had visited the Amery Ice Shelf — the longest ice shelf in the world. The team collected ice samples and data on temperatures, which are necessary for research on global warming. So far, about 27 countries have visited Antarctica for scientific research. Although the living conditions are very hard, many scientists have to stay there for long periods of time. So, how do they manage their lives on the ice? During the summer, the temperature in Antarctica reaches about −20℃. It falls to about −60℃ in winter. So, even if there are 24 hours of sunshine, scientists must keep wearing all the correct clothes to protect them from the cold. These clothes include jeans, running shoes, jackets, long underwear, boots and woolen socks. Although highly technical clothing provides much protection against the extreme cold, scientists often need to go outside when there is an icy wind blowing and the temperature is −30℃. Natural protection such as facial hair can also help. "That's why many researchers wear a beard. It really does keep you warm," says German explorer Arved Fuchs. Usually, the polar researchers have good meals. Some even have feasts on holidays like Christmas and New Year's Day. Vegetables are always welcomed and usually finished the quickest. Life on the ice means living with other researchers in tight living spaces. Most people sleep in dorm-style rooms. More remote field camps use separate tents. So, at least some researchers don't have to put up with annoying snorers.

Questions 13 to 15 are based on the passage you have just heard.

13. Why did researchers visit Amery Ice Shelf?

14. What is the matter that researchers care most for living in Antarctica?

15. What best describes the living space of most researchers on the Amery Ice Shelf?

◇ Section C

• Recording One

In the not-so distant past, most people thought that when a woman reached her 40s, it was too late for her to have children. The time on her biological clock had run out. Well, that has changed. These days some women are resetting their biological clocks. They are giving themselves more time to have children. Make no mistake. Being a "Single Mother by Choice" is very different from younger women who find themselves pregnant, perhaps not by choice. Generally speaking, single mothers by choice are older and well educated. They are usually financially secure and successful in their careers. So, they have the money. What they may not have is a partner. These women find themselves in their late 30s or early 40s, single and wanting children. This is the place in life where writer Kerry Reichs found herself several years ago. She says she did not plan to become a single mother. She says she just did not find the right partner. "Well, you certainly don't wake up when you're a ten-year-old girl and think,' Someday I want to be a single mother all by myself.' So I think I had a set of standards for the partner I was looking for and I didn't meet anyone who fit those standards. And, at 39 I found myself single, without children and I wanted them very much. So, I decided to do this on my own." he says it was a difficult decision. It meant giving up on the idea, the fantasy, of having the "perfect" family. In the end, she decided that she had the resources and the temperament, or mental ability to do it. Kerry Reichs chose to get pregnant from an anonymous sperm donor. She says the experience was surreal, too strange to be real. There have also been changes in U.S. public opinion toward unmarried women having children. There is no longer a social stigma on a woman having a baby without a partner. But single mothers by choice do have their critics. Conservative groups and social commentators say that choosing to become a single mom is not good for the child, families or society. However, according to Kerry Reichs, this is not a decision women come to easily. She says for many if not most women this is a decision of last resort, meaning there are no other choices for them. There apparently still exists a lot to explore and discuss, but one thing is sure: "Single Mother By Choice" opens up a new possibility for women today with new conceptions of family.

Questions 16 to 19 are based on the recording you have just heard.

16. In the past, what did people think of women in their 40s?

17. How does "Single Mother By Choice" differ from younger women who're pregnant unplanned?

18. Why did Kerry Reichs decide to become a "single mother by choice"?

19. What is the U. S. public opinion toward single mothers by choice?

· **Recording Two**

A new study has found that excessive alcohol drinking costs Americans more than 220 billion dollars a year. That amount is equal to almost two dollars a drink. But study organizers believe the biggest costs come from a loss of worker productivity. Robert Brewer works for America's Centers for Disease Control and Prevention, a public health agency. He helped to produce a report on the study. The researchers used findings from 2006 to examine different costs linked to heavy drinking. They looked at results from around the United States and found a lot of variation in different parts of the country. Alcohol-related costs include health care, the cost of trying cases for drinking-related crimes and property damage from road accidents. Robert Brewer says the biggest cost is lost productivity. Many people with a drinking problem have lower-paying jobs. He says they may also be less productive when they are at work. "In addition to that, a number of people die of alcohol-attributable conditions, and many of those folks die in the prime of their life. So there is the personal tragedy there, but there is also a huge economic cost to somebody dying, for example, in an alcohol-related motor vehicle crash at age 35." The researchers were mainly concerned about the cost of heavy alcohol use. The study didn't look at the effect on individuals who drink a glass of beer or wine with dinner. Mr. Brewer says the largest costs come from binge drinking when people drink a lot of alcohol in a short period of time. The study was based on the economic costs of heavy drinking in the United States. But Mr. Brewer says many nations have problems with what the World Health Organization calls "harmful use of alcohol". "But I think that it is very reasonable to assume that harmful alcohol use is gonna result in some of the same consequences in other countries, even if the cost associated with those consequences are different." The study on the economic costs of excessive alcohol use was published in the American Journal of Preventive Medicine. Two years ago, a British medical examiner ruled that singer Amy Winehouse died as a result of drinking too much alcohol. Winehouse was only 27 years old. Tests showed that she died after drinking enough alcohol to put her blood alcohol level at more than five times the legal drunk—driving limit. The award-winning singer had a well-documented battle with drugs and alcohol. I'm Christopher Cruise. Thank you for listening.

Questions 20 to 22 are based on the recording you have just heard.

20. What do researchers believe to be the biggest alcohol-related cost?

21. What did Robert Brewer say about the "harmful use of alcohol"?

22. What do we learn about Amy Winehouse?

• **Recording Three**

Hi everybody. I'm speaking with you from the D.C. Public Library in Anacostia, where I just met with a group of promising middle school students. We spent some time talking about their lives, and how we all care about their success — and how that starts with a good education. So one thing I announced here in Anacostia is a new project by libraries and major publishers to provide more than $250 million in free e-Books for low-income students. We also issued a challenge to mayors, libraries, and school leaders to help every student get a library card, so they can expand their horizons in a place like this. It's all part of our connected initiative to connect 99% of America's students to high-speed Internet. Because no matter who you are, where you live, or how much money you've got, you should be able to access the world's knowledge and information just like anyone else. In a global economy, we've got to help ensure that everyone, of every age, in every zip code — urban and rural — has the chance to learn the skills that lead directly to a good job. That's also why I've put forward a plan to make two years of community college as free and universal for every American as high school is today. It's something I'll talk about in my commencement address next week at Lake Area Tech, in the small town of Watertown, South Dakota. It's a community college with a graduation rate that is nearly twice the national average. They're proving that a great education can be within everyone's reach. All of us have a responsibility to not only make sure our own children have pathways to success but that all children do. And a great education is the ticket to a better life like never before. Making sure all our kids receive one is the surest way to show them that their lives matter. And it's the smartest way to prove to them that in communities like this, and in a country like ours, we believe in opportunity for all. Thanks, everybody. And have a great weekend.

Questions 23 to 25 are based on the recording you have just heard.

23. What does the new project aim to achieve?

24. What did the lecturer say about the plan about community college?

25. What does a great education mean to children?

■ Chapter 6

· **Compound Dictation One**

A Visual History of Social Dance in 25 Moves

This is the Bop. The Bop is a type of social dance.

Dance is a language, and social dance is an expression that emerges from a community. A social dance isn't choreographed by any one person. It can't be traced to any one moment.

Each dance has steps that everyone can agree on, but it's about the individual and their creative identity. Because of that, social dances bubble up, they change and they spread like wildfire.

They are as old as our remembered history. In African-American social dances, we see over 200 years of how African and African-American traditions influenced our history. The present always contains the past. And the past shapes who we are and who we will be.

The Juba dance was born from enslaved Africans' experience on the plantation. Brought to the Americas, stripped of a common spoken language, this dance was a way for enslaved Africans to remember where they're from. It may have looked something like this.

Slapping thighs, shuffling feet and patting hands: this was how they got around the slave owners' ban on drumming, improvising complex rhythms just like ancestors did with drums in Haiti or in the Yoruba communities of West Africa. It was about keeping cultural traditions alive and retaining a sense of inner freedom under captivity.

It was the same subversive spirit that created this dance: the Cakewalk, a dance that parodied the mannerisms of Southern high society — a way for the enslaved to throw shade at the masters. The crazy thing about this dance is that the Cakewalk was performed for the masters, who never suspected they were being made fun of.

Now you might recognize this one, 1920s — the Charleston. The Charleston was all about improvisation and musicality, making its way into Lindy Hop, swing dancing and even the Kid n Play, originally called the Funky Charleston.

Started by a tight-knit Black community near Charleston, South Carolina, the Charleston permeated dance halls where young women suddenly had the freedom to kick their heels and move their legs.

Now, social dance is about community and connection; if you knew the steps, it meant you belonged to a group. But what if it becomes a worldwide craze? Enter the Twist. It's no surprise that the Twist can be traced back to the 19th century, brought to America from the Congo during slavery. But in the late '50s, right before the Civil Rights Movement, the Twist is popularized by Chubby Checker and Dick Clark. Suddenly, everybody's doing the Twist: white teenagers, kids in Latin America, making its way into songs and movies. Through social dance, the boundaries between groups become blurred.

The story continues in the 1980s and '90s. Along with the emergence of hip-hop, African-American social dance took on even more visibility, borrowing from its long past, shaping culture and being shaped by it.

Today, these dances continue to evolve, grow and spread.

Why do we dance? To move, to let loose, to express. Why do we dance together? To heal, to remember, to say: "We speak a common language. We exist and we are free."

- **Compound Dictation Two**

The Playful Wonderland behind Great Inventions

Roughly 43,000 years ago, a young cave bear died in the rolling hills on the northwest border of modern day Slovenia. A thousand years later, a mammoth died in southern Germany. A few centuries after that, a griffon vulture also died in the same vicinity. And we know almost nothing about how these animals met their deaths, but these different creatures dispersed across both time and space did share one remarkable fate. After their deaths, a bone from each of their skeletons was crafted by human hands into a flute.

Think about that for a second. Imagine you're a caveman, 40,000 years ago. You've mastered fire. You've built simple tools for hunting. You've learned how to craft garments from animal skins to keep yourself warm in the winter. What would you choose to invent next? It seems preposterous that you would invent the flute, a tool that created useless vibrations in air molecules. But that is exactly what our ancestors did.

Now this turns out to be surprisingly common in the history of innovation. Sometimes people invent things because they want to stay alive or feed their children or conquer the village next door. But just as often, new ideas come into the world simply because they're fun. And here's the really strange thing: many of those playful but seemingly frivolous inventions ended up sparking momentous transformations in science, in politics and society.

Take what may be the most important invention of modern times: programmable computers. Now, the standard story is that computers descend from military technology, since many of the early computers were designed specifically to crack wartime codes or calculate rocket trajectories. But in fact, the origins of the modern computer are much more playful, even musical, than you might imagine. The idea behind the flute, of just pushing air through tubes to make a sound, was eventually modified to create the first organ more than 2,000 years ago. Someone came up with the brilliant idea of triggering sounds by pressing small levers with our fingers, inventing the first musical keyboard. Now, keyboards evolved from organs to clavichords to harpsichords to the piano, until the middle of the 19th century, when a bunch of inventors finally hit on the idea of using a keyboard to trigger not sounds but letters. In fact, the very first typewriter was originally called "the writing harpsichord."

Flutes and music led to even more powerful breakthroughs. About a thousand years ago, at the height of the Islamic Renaissance, three brothers in Baghdad designed a device that was an automated organ. They called it "the instrument that plays itself." Now, the instrument was basically a giant music box. The organ could be trained to play various songs by using instructions encoded by placing pins on a rotating cylinder. And if you wanted the machine to play a different song, you just swapped a new cylinder in with a different code on it. This instrument was the first of its kind. It was programmable.

Now, conceptually, this was a massive leap forward. The whole idea of hardware and software becomes thinkable for the first time with this invention. And that incredibly powerful concept didn't come to us as an instrument of war or of conquest, or necessity at all. It came from the strange delight of watching a machine play music.

In fact, the idea of programmable machines was exclusively kept alive by music for about 700 years. In the 1700s, music-making machines became the playthings of the Parisian elite. Showmen used the same coded cylinders to control the physical movements of what were called automata, an early kind of robot. One of the most famous of those robots was, you guessed it, an automated flute player designed by a brilliant French inventor named Jacques de Vaucanson.

And as de Vaucanson was designing his robot musician, he had another idea. If you could program a machine to make pleasing sounds, why not program it to weave delightful patterns of color out of cloth? Instead of using the pins of the cylinder to represent musical notes, they would represent threads with different colors. If you wanted a new pattern for your fabric, you just programmed a new cylinder. This was the first programmable loom.

Now, the cylinders were too expensive and time-consuming to make, but a half century later, another French inventor named Jacquard hit upon the brilliant idea of using paper-punched cards instead of metal cylinders. Paper turned out to be much cheaper and more flexible as a way of programming the device. That punch card system inspired Victorian inventor Charles Babbage to create his analytical engine, the first true programmable computer ever designed. And punch cards were used by computer programmers as late as the 1970s.

So ask yourself this question: what really made the modern computer possible? Yes, the military involvement is an important part of the story, but inventing a computer also required other building blocks: music boxes, toy robot flute players, harpsichord keyboards, colorful patterns woven into fabric, and that's just a small part of the story. There's a long list of world-changing ideas and technologies that came out of play: public museums, rubber, probability theory, the insurance business and many more.

Necessity isn't always the mother of invention. The playful state of mind is fundamentally exploratory, seeking out new possibilities in the world around us. And that seeking is why so many experiences that started with simple delight and amusement eventually led us to profound breakthroughs.

Now, I think this has implications for how we teach kids in school and how we encourage innovation in our workspaces, but thinking about play and delight this way also helps us detect what's coming next. Think about it: if you were sitting there in 1750 trying to figure out the big changes coming to society in the 19th, the 20th centuries, automated machines, computers, artificial intelligence, a programmable flute entertaining the Parisian elite would have been as powerful a clue as anything else at the time. It seemed like an amusement at best, not useful in any serious way, but it turned out to be the beginning of a tech revolution that would change the world.

You'll find the future wherever people are having the most fun.

- *Video Appreciation:4 Reasons to Learn a New Language*

The language I'm speaking right now is on its way to becoming the world's universal language, for better or for worse. Let's face it, it's the language of the internet, it's the language of finance, it's the language of air traffic control, of popular music, diplomacy — English is everywhere.

Now, Mandarin Chinese is spoken by more people, but more Chinese people are learning English than English speakers are learning Chinese. Last I heard, there are two dozen universities in China right now teaching all in English. English is taking over.

And in addition to that, it's been predicted that at the end of the century almost all of the languages that exist now — there are about 6,000 — will no longer be spoken. There will only be some hundreds left. And on top of that, it's at the point where instant translation of live speech is not only possible, but it gets better every year.

The reason I'm reciting those things to you is because I can tell that we're getting to the point where a question is going to start being asked, which is: Why should we learn foreign languages — other than if English happens to be foreign to one? Why bother to learn another one when it's getting to the point where almost everybody in the world will be able to communicate in one?

I think there are a lot of reasons, but I first want to address the one that you're probably most likely to have heard of, because actually it's more dangerous than you might think. And that is the idea that a language channels your thoughts, that the vocabulary and the grammar of different languages gives everybody a different kind of acid trip, so to speak. That is a marvelously enticing idea, but it's kind of fraught.

So it's not that it's untrue completely. So for example, in French and Spanish the word for table is, for some reason, marked as feminine. So, "la table," "la mesa," you just have to deal with it. It has been shown that if you are a speaker of one of those languages and you happen to be asked how you would imagine a table talking, then much more often than could possibly be an accident, a French or a Spanish speaker says that the table would talk with a high and feminine voice. So if you're French or Spanish, to you, a table is kind of a girl, as opposed to if you are an English speaker.

It's hard not to love data like that, and many people will tell you that that means that there's a worldview that you have if you speak one of those languages. But you have to watch out, because imagine if somebody put us under the microscope, the us being those of us who speak English natively. What is the worldview from English?

So for example, let's take an English speaker. Up on the screen, that is Bono. He speaks English. I presume he has a worldview. Now, that is Donald Trump. In his way, he speaks English as well.

And here is Ms. Kardashian, and she is an English speaker, too. So here are three speakers of the English language. What worldview do those three people have in common? What worldview is shaped through the English language that unites them? It's a highly fraught concept. And so gradual consensus is becoming that language can shape thought, but it tends to be in rather darling, obscure psychological flutters. It's not a matter of giving you a different pair of glasses on the world.

Now, if that's the case, then why learn languages? If it isn't going to change the way you think, what would the other reasons be? There are some. One of them is that if you want to imbibe a culture, if you want to drink it in, if you want to become part of it, then whether or not the language channels the culture — and that seems doubtful — if you want to imbibe the culture, you have to control to some degree the language that the culture happens to be conducted in. There's no other way.

There's an interesting illustration of this. I have to go slightly obscure, but really you should seek it out. There's a movie by the Canadian film director Denys Arcand — read out in English on the page, "Dennis Arcand," if you want to look him up. He did a film called "Jesus of Montreal." And many of the characters are vibrant, funny, passionate, interesting French-Canadian, French-speaking women. There's one scene closest to the end, where they have to take a friend to an Anglophone hospital. In the hospital, they have to speak English. Now, they speak English but it's not their native language, they'd rather not speak English. And they speak it more slowly, they have accents, they're not idiomatic. Suddenly these characters that you've fallen in love with become husks of themselves, they're shadows of themselves.

To go into a culture and to only ever process people through that kind of skirm curtain is to never truly get the culture. And so to the extent that hundreds of languages will be left, one reason to learn them is because they are tickets to being able to participate in the culture of the people who speak them, just by virtue of the fact that it is their code. So that's one reason.

Second reason: it's been shown that if you speak two languages, dementia is less likely to set in, and that you are probably a better multitasker. And these are factors that set in early, and so that ought to give you some sense of when to give junior or juniorette lessons in another language. Bilingualism is healthy.

And then, third — languages are just an awful lot of fun. Much more fun than we're often told. So for example, Arabic: "kataba," he wrote, "yaktubu," he writes, she writes. "Uktub," write, in the imperative. What do those things have in common? All those things have in common the consonants sitting in the middle like pillars. They stay still, and the vowels dance around the consonants. Who wouldn't want to roll that around in their mouths? You can get that from Hebrew, you can get that from Ethiopia's main language, Amharic. That's fun. Or languages have different word orders. Learning how to speak with different word order is like driving on the different side of a street if you go to certain country, or the feeling that you get when you put Witch Hazel around your eyes and you feel the tingle. A language can do that to you.

So for example, "The Cat in the Hat Comes Back," a book that I'm sure we all often return to, like "Moby Dick." One phrase in it is, "Do you know where I found him? Do you know where he was? He was eating cake in the tub, Yes he was!" Fine. Now, if you learn that in Mandarin Chinese, then you have to master, "You can know, I did where him find? He was tub inside gorging cake, No mistake gorging chewing!" That just feels good. Imagine being able to do that for years and years at a time.

Or, have you ever learned any Cambodian? Me either, but if I did, I would get to roll around in my mouth not some baker's dozen of vowels like English has, but a good 30 different vowels scooching and oozing around in the Cambodian mouth like bees in a hive. That is what a language can get you.

And more to the point, we live in an era when it's never been easier to teach yourself another language. It used to be that you had to go to a classroom, and there would be some diligent teacher — some genius teacher in there — but that person was only in there at certain times and you had to go then, and then was not most times. You had to go to class. If you didn't have that, you had something called a record. I cut my teeth on those. There was only so much data on a record, or a cassette, or even that antique object known as a CD. Other than that you had books that didn't work, that's just the way it was.

Today you can lay down — lie on your living room floor, sipping bourbon, and teach yourself any language that you want to with wonderful sets such as Rosetta Stone. I highly recommend the lesser known Glossika as well. You can do it any time, therefore you can do it more and better. You can give yourself your morning pleasures in various languages. I take some "Dilbert" in various languages every single morning; it can increase your skills. Couldn't have done it 20 years ago when the idea of having any language you wanted in your pocket, coming from your phone, would have sounded like science fiction to very sophisticated people.

So I highly recommend that you teach yourself languages other than the one that I'm speaking, because there's never been a better time to do it. It's an awful lot of fun. It won't change your mind, but it will most certainly blow your mind. Thank you very much.

◇ Section A

- **Conversation One**

M: I see your new resume that you worked as a manager of a store called Computer Country. Could you tell me a little more about your responsibilities there?

W: Sure. I was responsible for overseeing about 30 employees. I did all of the ordering for the store and I kept track of the inventory.

M: What was the most difficult part of your job?

W: Probably handling angry customers. We didn't have them very often, but when we did, I needed to make sure they were well taken care of. After all, the customer is always right.

M: That's how we feel here, too. How long did you work there?

W: I was there for 3-and-a-half years. I left the company last month.

M: And why did you leave?

W: My husband has been transferred to Boston and I understand your company has an opening there, too.

M: Yes, that's right. We do. But the position won't start until early next month. Would that be a problem for you?

W: No, not at all. My husband's new job doesn't begin for a few weeks, so we thought we would spend some time driving to Boston and stop to see my parents.

M: That sounds nice. So, tell me, why are you interested in this particular position?

W: I know that your company has a great reputation and a wonderful product. I've thought many times that I would like to be a part of it. When I heard about the opening in Boston, I jumped to the opportunity.

M: Well, I'm glad you did.

Questions 1 to 4 are based on the conversation you have just heard.

1. What was the woman's previous job?
2. What does the woman say with the most difficult part of her job?
3. Why is the woman looking for a job in Boston?
4. When can the woman start to work if she gets the job?

- **Conversation Two**

W: Today, in this studio, we have Alberto Cuties, the well-known Brazilian advocator of the anti-global movement. He's here to talk about the recent report stating that by 2050,

Brazil will be one of the world's wealthiest and most successful countries. Alberto, what do you say to this report?

M: You know this isn't the first time that people are saying Brazil will be a great economic power. The same thing was said over 100 years ago, but it didn't happen.

W: Yes, but you must admit the world's a very different place now.

M: Of course. In fact, I believe that there may be some truth in the predictions this time around. First of all, though, we must remember the problems facing Brazil at the moment.

W: Such as?

M: There's an enormous gap between the rich and the poor in this country. In San Paulo, you can see shopping malls full of designer goods right next door to the slum areas without proper water or electricity supplies. A lot of work needs to be done to help people in those areas improve their lives.

W: What needs to be done?

M: Education, for example. For Brazil, to be successful, we need to offer education to all Brazilians. Successful countries, like South Korea and Singapore, have excellent education systems. Brazil needs to learn from these countries.

W: So you're hopeful for the future?

W: As I said earlier, I'm hopeful. This isn't an easy job. We need to make sure that these important opportunities for Brazil aren't wasted as they were in the past.

Questions 5 to 8 are based on the conversation you have just heard.

5. What does the recent report say about Brazil?

6. What problem does Alberto say Brazil faces now?

7. What does Alberto say about economically successful countries?

8. What is Alberto's attitude towards Brazil's future?

◇ Section B

• Passage One

Wilma Subra had no intention of becoming a public speaker. After graduating from college with degrees in chemistry and microbiology, she went to work at Gulf South Research Institute in Louisiana. As part of her job, she conducted field research on toxic substances in the environment, often in minority communities located near large industrial polluters. She found many families were being exposed to high, sometimes deadly levels of chemicals and other toxic substances. But she was not allowed to make her information public. Frustrated by these restrictions, Subra left her job in 1981, created her own company and has devoted the past two decades to helping people fight back against giant industrial polluters. She works with families and community groups to conduct environmental tests, interpret test results, and organize for change. Because of her efforts, dozens of toxic sites across the country have been cleaned up. And one chemical industry spokesperson calls her "a top gun" for the environmental movement. How has Subra achieved all this? Partly through her scientific training, partly through her commitment to environmental justice. But just as important is her ability to communicate with people through public speaking. "Public speaking," she says, "is the primary vehicle I use for reaching people." If you had asked Subra before 1981, "do you see yourself as a major public speaker?" She would have laughed at the idea. Yet today she gives more than 100 presentations a year. Along the way, she's lectured at Harvard, testified before congress, and addressed audiences in 40 states, as well as in Mexico, Canada, and Japan.

Questions 9 to 12 are based on the passage you have just heard.

9. What did Wilma Subra do as part of her job on working at Gulf South Research Institute?

10. Why did Wilma Subra leave her job in 1981?

11. What results have Wilma Subra's efforts had in the past two decades?

12. What does the speaker say has contributed to Wilma Subra's success?

· **Passage Two**

One of the biggest challenges facing employers and educators today is the rapid advance of globalization. The market place is no longer national or regional, but extends to all corners of the world. And this requires a global-ready workforce. Universities have a large part to play in preparing students for the 21st century labor market by promoting international educational experiences. The most obvious way universities can help develop a global workforce is by encouraging students to study abroad as part of their course. Students who have experienced another culture firsthand are more likely to be global-ready when they graduate. Global workforce development doesn't always have to involve travel abroad, however. If students learn another language and study other cultures, they will be more global-ready when they graduate. It is important to point out that students also need to have a deep understanding of their own culture before they can begin to observe, analyze and evaluate other cultures. In multi-cultural societies, people can study each other's cultures to develop intercultural competencies, such as critical and reflective thinking and intellectual flexibility. This can be done both through the curriculum and through activities on campus outside of the classroom, such as art exhibitions and lectures from international experts. Many universities are already embracing this challenge and providing opportunities for students to become global citizens. Students themselves, however, may not realize that when they graduate, they will be competing in a global labor market. And universities need to raise awareness of these issues amongst undergraduates.

Questions 13 to 15 are based on the passage you have just heard.

13. What is one of the biggest challenges facing employers and educators today?

14. What should students do first before they can really understand other cultures?

15. What should college students realize according to the speaker?

◇ Section C

• **Recording One**

Good morning, I'm Anna Matteo. If you are a man living in China and smoke, you may want to stop. That is because one in three of all the young men in China will die from smoking cigarettes or other tobacco products. Researchers reported their findings in The Lancet Medical Journal. The report says, "About two-thirds of young Chinese men become cigarette smokers, and most start before they are 20 years old. Unless they stop, about half of them will eventually be killed by their habit." The researchers conducted two large, countrywide studies on the health effects of smoking. The first study took place in the 1990s and involved about 250,000 men. The second study was launched only recently and is continuing. This study involves about 500,000 adults, both men and women. Researchers say that in China, the number of deaths each year resulting from tobacco use will rise from about one million in 2010 to two million in 2030. They warn that the number will rise to three-million by 2050. Researchers say there is no silver bullet to make these numbers go down, meaning there is no easy answer to make the problem go away. People need to stop smoking. China smokes more than one-third of the world's cigarettes. It also has one-sixth of all smoking-related deaths worldwide. The story is different with Chinese women. It seems not many women are smoking in China today. Ten percent of women born in the 1930s were smokers. But among those born in the 1960s, only about one percent smoke. And the rates of death-by-cigarette among women have also dropped. But that could change. Researchers note that smoking now seems more fashionable among Chinese women. Some women think it makes them seem more appealing. Richard Peto is a professor at the University of Oxford. He helped to write the report on smoking. He said increasing the price of cigarettes may be one way to reduce smoking rates. He said, "Over the past 20 years, tobacco deaths have been decreasing in Western countries, partly because of price increases." For China, he added, a large increase in cigarette prices could save tens of millions of lives. More information about Richard Peto can be found on the University of Oxford website. There it says Richard Peto's investigations into the worldwide health effects of smoking have helped to change "national and international attitudes about smoking and public health". He was the first to describe clearly the future worldwide health effects of current smoking patterns. Mr. Peto was knighted by Queen Elizabeth in 1999 for services to epidemiology. In 2010 and 2011 he received the Cancer Research UK and the British Medical Journal Lifetime Achievement

Award.

Questions 16 to 19 are based on the recording you have just heard.

16. What does the report say about Chinese male smokers?
17. What do the researchers say about reducing deaths from tobacco use in China?
18. What do we learn about smoking among Chinese women?
19. What is the contribution of Richard Peto?

- **Recording Two**

Our country is home to some of the most beautiful God-given landscapes in the world. We're blessed with natural treasures — from the Grand Tetons to the Grand Canyon; from lush forests and vast deserts to lakes and rivers abundantly filled with wildlife. And it's our responsibility to protect these treasures for future generations, just as previous generations protected them for us. I'm going to keep protecting the places that make America special, and the livelihoods of those who depend on them. We'll also keep doing what we can to prevent the worst effects of climate change before it's too late. Over the past six years, we've led by example, generating more clean energy and lowering our carbon emissions. Our businesses have stepped up in a big way, including just this past week. Some of our biggest companies made new commitments to act on climate — not just because it's good for the planet, but because it's good for their bottom line. This is how America is leading on the environment. And because America is leading by example, 150 countries, representing over 85% of global emissions, have now laid out plans to reduce their levels of the harmful carbon pollution that warms our planet. And it gives us great momentum going into Paris this December, where the world needs to come together and build on these individual commitments with an ambitious, long-term agreement to protect this Earth for our kids. Now Congress has to do its job. This month, even as Republicans in Congress barely managed to keep our government open, they shut down something called the Land and Water Conservation Fund. For more than half a century, this fund has protected more than 5 million acres of land—from playgrounds to parks to priceless landscapes—all without costing taxpayers a dime. Nearly every single county in America has benefited from this program. It has bipartisan support in both the House and the Senate. Republicans in Congress should reauthorize and fully fund the Land and Water Conservation Fund without delay. After all, as Pope Francis reminds us so eloquently, this planet is a gift from God — and our common home. We should leave it to our kids in better shape than we found it.

Questions 20 to 22 are based on the recording you have just heard.

20. What have been done to prevent the worst effects of climate change?
21. What is the effect of America's action on protecting the environment?
22. What do we learn about the Land and Water Conservation Fund?

• Recording Three

Good evening and welcome to tonight's program. Our guest is the world-known Dr. Charles Adams, who has sparked a great deal of attention over the past several years for his research in the area of language learning. His new book Learning a Language over Eggs and Toast has been on the best seller list for the past six weeks. Welcome to our program. Dr. Adams: Ah, it's a pleasure to be here. Well, one of the most important keys to learning another language is to establish a regular study program, like planning a few minutes every morning around breakfast time. I'm not implying that we can become fluent speakers in a matter of a few minutes here and there, but rather a regular, consistent, and focused course of study can help us on the way to the promised language of language mastery, and remember there is a difference between native fluency and proficiency in a language, and I am proposing the latter. People need to plan out their study by setting realistic and attainable goals from the beginning. I mean, some people get caught up in the craze of learning the language in 30 days, only to become disinterested when they don't perform up their expectations. And small steps, little by little, are the key. For example, planning to learn five new vocabulary words a day and to learn to use them actively is far better than learning 30 and forgetting them the next day. People often have different ways of learning and approach learning tasks differently. Some people are visual learners who prefer to see models of the patterns they are expected to learn; others are auditory learners who favor hearing instructions, for example over reading them. Now, our preferences are determined by many factors for example, personality, culture, and past experience. I am a very tactile learner which means I learn through hands-on experience. Moving around while trying to learn and memorize material helps me a great deal. While I cut up tomatoes and onions for my omelet in the morning, I might recite aloud vocabulary to the rhythm of the knife. But it is important to remember that often our learning styles are not singular in nature, but are often very multidimensional, and we tend to learn differently in different situations. For more on language learning, you will have to read my book to find out.

Questions 23 to 25 are based on the recording you have just heard.

23. What is one of the most important keys to learning another language?

24. What do we know about people's ways of learning?

25. What does the speaker say about people's learning styles?

■ Chapter 7

• Compound Dictation One

Different Meanings of Words in Britain and America

Please welcome David Williams and Ben Stiller.

D (David Williams): Good evening. My name is David Williams and I am a British.

B (Ben Stiller): Hi, I'm Ben Stiller and I'm an American. USA USA USA USA!

D: Amnesty International has invited us here this evening to explain the different meanings of words in Britain and America to help strengthen the union between our two nations.

B: The first word is jugs.

D: In Britain, this is a container with a sprout and handle for pouring liquid.

B: Tits.

D: Next is hooters. For the British, these are steam whistles in a factory that signal the cessation of work.

B: Tits again.

D: Aluminium, a silvery white metal.

B: Aluminum, a silvery white metal.

D: It's aluminium.

B: It's aluminum.

D: Alumin- i – u – m.

B: Alumin – um.

D: I – u – m.

B: um.

D: A la mode, from the French, on the fashion.

B: With ice-cream.

D: Passport, an official government document that permits a citizen to travel abroad.

B: We don't have that word in America.

B: Dentist, a person trained to look after the healthy appearance of your teeth.

D: We don't have that word in Britain.

D: Obese, anyone over 200 pounds.

D: Anyone over 2000 pounds.

D: Blue steel, a British airforce missile.

D: In America?

D: Piers Morgan, an annoying man who used to be on TV in Britain.

B: An annoying man who is on TV in America.

D: Bush, a private part that is too embarrassing to mention.

B: Same in here then.

D: Sudden death penalty shootout, a way of settling scores in soccer.

B: A way of settling scores in Texas.

B: Voice mail, a place where friends or family members leave messages for you to listen to later.

D: A place where friends or family members leave messages for journalists to listen to later.

D: Harry Potter, a fictional boy wizard who goes to Hogwarts School.

B: Fictional?

D: Yeah, of course. Harry Potter is fictional.

B: OK. But the Quidditch thing, that's real, right?

D: No, no, you know, it's made up, it's fantasy, like Night in the Museum.

B: Night in the museum isn't real?

D: Our final word tonight is Ass, a donkey.

B: Buttocks/ boody/ junk in the trunk/ bubble/ dookie maker…

D: Yes, thank you. We get the picture.

B: I think you'll agree, my British friend, that we Americans knew Brits really do speak the same language.

D: No, we don't.

B: It's alumin – um.

D: Shut up!

• Compound Dictation Two

The British and the American

When I came to study abroad in England, I pretty much thought that it would be like living in the U.S. but with English accents. I mean we both speak the same language basically, but everything else between the English people and the American is basically completely different. And it's not just the fact that they use mint jelly as a condiment or that they drink tea every hour every day. It's the little things, like asking "How are you", for example. In the U.S., when we ask someone how they are we say:"How are you?" In England, it's a little different. They say, "You alright?", which…is weird because in the U.S. usually when you ask someone if you are alright, it implies that they don't look alright. So every time someone in England ask me "You alright?" I always have to like three seconds introspection about whether or not I look miserable or not, and then I'm very intelligible saying something like "Yeah, I mean…yes. I am alright." "Uh…are you alright?" and then there is a whole knife thing. Since I move here for three months, I went to Poundland and bought kitchen's supplies because I don't really need them last long. But what I didn't expect, when I got to the counter was that the cashier will take out the knife and hold it up as if I were trying to buy illicit drugs or something from her. I just remember her looking at me, and then asking for my ID, which she looked at for 20 seconds before she called her manager. So the manager comes over, and he spends a good 30 seconds looking at my picture on my license, comparing it to me. And meanwhile I am standing there, contemplating whether or not I should crush out of the Poundland window like I am Channing Tatum way to house down or something. But I keep it cool, and the manager gives you, ok, I am allowed to purchase the knife. I'm sorry. But if you like U.K., should learn Americans this kind of thing. Because when you grow up in a country where the cashier in Walmart asks if you want your complementary shot gun in your bag or not, It's alarming to get 30 degree for trying to buy a knife that can barely cut a baby carrot! Speaking of eating, English people seem to have a different concept of what counts as "travel food". Americans are big fan into walking and drinking. If it's not a cup of cappuccino, it's coke, a Gatorade or maybe even the water stuff that people are talking about. But here in England, it's sandwiches. People in England like sandwiches. It's like no matter where you are and what time it is, someone is walking around eating a sandwich or like these pastry things which basically look like fat hot pocket. Every few feet in England there is a somewhere to buy a sandwich. You can even buy sandwiches in the freaking beauty store. But maybe even more bizarre is how unfearful English drivers are when they come to pedestrians. They will run you over. There is about a 0% chance that someone will stop it they see you in the middle of the street even if it is a mother, pushing her baby across the street in a crossroad. A car will literally wait to the last possible second before slamming on their breaks and blowing their honk. Honestly though the strangest thing that I have encountered in the UK is side walk. In the U.S. we drive on the right so technically you're side supposed to walk at the right of the side walk. So you would think that because English people drive on the left, they will walk on the left side of the side walk. You will be wrong. I can now tell you how many times I have been walking down at the left side of the side walk here when the person coming towards me, will slowly drift to the right hand side right directly in front of me. This generally leads to like this awkward "oh, sorry" thing before I have to move to the right to let them pass. But eve more strange, if there are a group of people taking up the whole side walk and you are walking towards them, 80% of time they will make no effort what's so ever to let you pass. I felt people almost push me into the oncoming traffic because they are so unwilling t move to the left side of the side walk to let me pass. All I am saying is you make your choice in England. You guys wrote like "Hey guys, let's drive on the left hand side of the road", so left hand side is your side. You can't decide to walk at the right side of the sidewalk. That just…it's not cool. If you want to walk at the right side on the side walk, then the escalator should go the right way and you should drive on the right hand side of the road. (sigh)

Put all my judgments aside, I really do love here in England. I like the fact that you can go and buy a good sandwich at the drug store and running outdoor, here has pretty much satisfied my urge of ever wanting to run across a Martio car track. So…I think it's a win-win either way. It may be a lot of things I don't understand here, and in two weeks when I leave, there're still gonna be things that I don't understand. But I am very glad that I got a chance to experience them. And…that's your happy ending for you. I have nothing else. Cheers!

• *Video Appreciation: Why I Keep Speaking up, even When People Mock My Accent?*

I used to have this recurring dream where I'd walk into a roomful of people, and I'd try not to make eye contact with anyone. Until someone notices me, and I just panic. And the person walks up to me, and says, "Hi, my name is so-and-so. And what is your name?" And I'm just quiet, unable to respond. After some awkward silence, he goes, "Have you forgotten your name?" And I'm still quiet. And then, slowly, all the other people in the room begin to turn toward me and ask, almost in unison,

(Voice-over, several voices) "Have you forgotten your name?" As the chant gets louder, I want to respond, but I don't.

I'm a visual artist. Some of my work is humorous, and some is a bit funny but in a sad way.

And one thing that I really enjoy doing is making these little animations where I get to do the voice-over for all kinds of characters. I've been a bear.

(Video) Bear (Safwat Saleem's voice): Hi.

(Laughter)

Safwat Saleem: I've been a whale.

(Video) Whale (SS's voice): Hi.

(Laughter)

SS: I've been a greeting card.

(Video) Greeting card (SS's voice): Hi.

(Laughter)

SS: And my personal favorite is Frankenstein's monster.

(Video) Frankenstein's monster (SS's voice): (Grunts)

(Laughter)

SS: I just had to grunt a lot for that one.

A few years ago, I made this educational video about the history of video games. And for that one, I got to do the voice of Space Invader.

(Video) Space Invader (SS's voice): Hi.

SS: A dream come true, really, (Laughter) And when that video was posted online, I just sat there on the computer, hitting "refresh," excited to see the response. The first comment comes in.

(Video) Comment: Great job. SS: Yes! I hit "refresh."

(Video) Comment: Excellent video. I look forward to the next one.

SS: This was just the first of a two-part video. I was going to work on the second one next. I hit "refresh."

(Video) Comment: Where is part TWO? WHEREEEEE? I need it NOWWWWW!: P

(Laughter)

SS: People other than my mom were saying nice things about me, on the Internet! It felt like I had finally arrived. I hit "refresh."

(Video) Comment: His voice is annoying. No offense.

SS: OK, no offense taken. Refresh.

(Video) Comment: Could you remake this without peanut butter in your mouth?

SS: OK, at least the feedback is somewhat constructive. Hit "refresh."

(Video) Comment: Please don't use this narrator again. You can barely understand him.

SS: Refresh.

(Video) Comment: Couldn't follow because of the Indian accent.

SS: OK, OK, OK, two things. Number one, I don't have an Indian accent, I have a Pakistani accent, OK? And number two, I clearly have a Pakistani accent.(Laughter)But comments like that kept coming in, so I figured I should just ignore them and start working on the second part of the video. I recorded my audio, but every time I sat down to edit, I just could not do it. Every single time, it would take me back to my childhood, when I had a much harder time speaking.

I've stuttered for as long as I can remember. I was the kid in class who would never raise his hand when he had a question — or knew the answer. Every time the phone rang, I would run to the bathroom so I would not have to answer it. If it was for me, my parents would say I'm not around. I spent a lot of time in the bathroom. And I hated introducing myself, especially in groups. I'd always stutter on my name, and there was usually someone who'd go, "Have you forgotten your name?" And then everybody would laugh. That joke never got old. (Laughter)

I spent my childhood feeling that if I spoke, it would become obvious that there was something wrong with me, that I was not normal. So I mostly stayed quiet. And so you see, eventually for me to even be able to use my voice in my work was a huge step for me. Every time I record audio, I fumble my way through saying each sentence many, many times, and then I go back in and pick the ones where I think I suck the least.

(Voice-over) SS: Audio editing is like Photoshop for your voice. I can slow it down, speed it up, make it deeper, add an echo. And if I stutter along the way, and if I stutter along the way, I just go back in and fix it. It's magic.

SS: Using my highly edited voice in my work was a way for me to finally sound normal to myself. But after the comments on the video, it no longer made me feel normal. And so I stopped using my voice in my work. Since then, I've thought a lot about what it means to be normal. And I've come to understand that "normal" has a lot to do with expectations.

Let me give you an example. I came across this story about the Ancient Greek writer, Homer. Now, Homer mentions very few colors in his writing. And even when he does, he seems to get them quite a bit wrong. For example, the sea is described as wine red, people's faces are sometimes green and sheep are purple. But it's not just Homer. If you look at all of the ancient literature — Ancient Chinese, Icelandic, Greek, Indian and even the original Hebrew Bible — they all mention very few colors. And the most popular theory for why that might be the case is that cultures begin to recognize a color only once they have the ability to make that color. So basically, if you can make a color, only then can you see it. A color like red, which was fairly easy for many cultures to make — they began to see that color fairly early on. But a color like blue, which was much harder to make — many cultures didn't begin to learn how to make that color until much later. They didn't begin to see it until much later as well. So until then, even though a color might be all around them, they simply did not have the ability to see it. It was invisible. It was not a part of their normal.

And that story has helped put my own experience into context. So when I first read the comments on the video, my initial reaction was to take it all very personally. But the people commenting did not know how self-conscious I am about my voice. They were mostly reacting to my accent, that it is not normal for a narrator to have an accent.

But what is normal, anyway? We know that reviewers will find more spelling errors in your writing if they think you're black. We know that professors are less likely to help female or minority students. And we know that resumes with white-sounding names get more callbacks than resumes with black-sounding names. Why is that? Because of our expectations of what is normal. We think it is normal when a black student has spelling errors. We think it is normal when a female or minority student does not succeed. And we think it is normal that a white employee is a better hire than a black employee. But studies also show that discrimination of this kind, in most cases, is simply favoritism, and it results more from wanting to help people that you can relate to than the desire to harm people that you can't relate to.

And not relating to people starts at a very early age. Let me give you an example. One library that keeps track of characters in the children's book collection every year, found that in 2014, only about 11 percent of the books had a character of color. And just the year before, that number was about eight percent, even though half of American children today come from a minority background. Half.

So there are two big issues here. Number one, children are told that they can be anything, they can do anything, and yet, most stories that children of color consume are about people who are not like them. Number two is that majority groups don't get to realize the great extent to which they are similar to minorities — our everyday experiences, our hopes, our dreams, our fears and our mutual love for hummus. It's delicious!　(Laughter)

Just like the color blue for Ancient Greeks, minorities are not a part of what we consider normal, because normal is simply a construction of what we've been exposed to, and how visible it is around us.

And this is where things get a bit difficult. I can accept the preexisting notion of normal — that normal is good, and anything outside of that very narrow definition of normal is bad. Or I can challenge that preexisting notion of normal with my work and with my voice and with my accent and by standing here onstage, even though I'm scared shitless and would rather be in the bathroom. (Laughter) (Applause)

(Video) Sheep (SS's voice): I'm now slowly starting to use my voice in my work again. And it feels good. It does not mean I won't have a breakdown the next time a couple dozen people say that I talk (Mumbling) like I have peanut butter in my mouth. (Laughter)

SS: It just means I now have a much better understanding of what's at stake, and how giving up is not an option.

The Ancient Greeks didn't just wake up one day and realize that the sky was blue. It took centuries, even, for humans to realize what we had been ignoring for so long. And so we must continuously challenge our notion of normal, because doing so is going to allow us as a society to finally see the sky for what it is.

(Video) Characters: Thank you. Thank you. Thank you. Thank you. Thank you.
Frankenstein's monster: (Grunts) (Laughter)

SS: Thank you.　(Applause)

◇ **Section A**

1. W: The students have been protesting against the increased tuition.

M: Yeah, I heard about the protest. But I don't know how much good it will do.

Q: What does the man mean?

2. W: Jay will turn 21 this week. Does he know the classes are having a surprise party for him?

M: No, he thinks we are giving a party for the retiring dean.

Q: What do we learn from the conversation?

3. M: Hello, this is Carl's garage. We found Mr. White's briefcase and wallet after he left his car here this morning.

W: He has been wondering where he could have left them. I'll tell him to pick them up this afternoon. Thank you for calling.

Q: What do we learn about Mr. White from the conversation?

4. W: You know, some TV channels have been rerunning a lot of comedies from the 1960s'. What do you think of those old shows?

M: Not much. But the new ones including those done by famous directors are not so entertaining either.

Q: What does the man mean?

5. M: How much longer should I boil these vegetables? The recipe says about 10 minutes in total.

W: They look pretty done to me. I doubt you should cook them any more.

Q: What does the woman mean?

6. W: Tom, are you going to your parents' house tonight?

M: Yes, I promise to help them figure out their tax returns. The tax code is really confusing to them.

Q: What is the man going to do for his parents?

7. W: I was surprised when I heard you'd finished your research project a whole month early.

M: How I managed to do it is still a mystery to me.

Q: What does the man mean?

8. W: I was hoping we could be in the same developmental psychology class.

M: Me too, but by the time I went for registration the course was closed.

Q: What does the man mean?

· Long Conversation One

M: It's really amazing how many colors there are in these Thai silks.

W: These are our new designs.

M: Oh, I don't think I've seen this combination of colors before.

W: They're really brilliant, aren't they?

M: Quite dazzling! May I have samples of the new color combinations?

W: Yes, of course. But aren't you going to place an order?

M: We order them regularly, you know, but I do want our buyer who handles fabrics to see them.

W: Have you looked at the wood and stonecoverings? Did you like them?

M: Oh, they aren't really what I'm looking for.

W: What do you have in mind?

M: That's the trouble. I've never know exactly until I see it. I usually have more luck when I get away from the tourist places.

W: Out in the countryside you mean.

M: Yeah, exactly. Markets in small town shave turned out best for me.

W: You're more interested than in handicrafts that haven't been commercialized.

M: Yes, real folk arts, pots, dishes, basket ware — the kinds of things that people themselves use.

W: I'm sure we can arrange a trip out into the country for you.

M: I was hoping you'd say that.

W: We can drive out of Bangkok and stop whenever you see something that interests you.

M: That would be wonderful! How soon could we leave?

W: I can't get away tomorrow. But I think I can get a car for the day after.

M: And would we have to come back the same day?

W: No, I think I'll be able to keep the car for three or four days.

M: Wonderful! That'll give me time for a real look around.

Questions 9 to 11 are based on the conversation you have just heard.

9. What attracts the man to the Thai silks?

10. What is the man looking for in Thailand?

11. What do we learn about the trip the woman promised to arrange for the man?

• **Long Conversation Two**

W: Well, before we decide we're going to live in Enderby, we really ought to have a look at the schools; we want the children to have a good secondary education, so we'd better see what's available.

M: They gave me some information at the district office and I took notes. It appears there are five secondary schools in Enderby: three state schools and two private.

W: I don't know if we want private schools, do we?

M: I don't think so, but we'll look at them anyway. There's Saint Mary's, that's a Catholic school for girls, and Carlton Abbey— that's a very old boys' boarding school, founded in 1672.

W: Are all the state schools coeducational?

M: Yes, it seems so.

W: I think little Keith is going to be very good with his hands, we ought to send him to a school with good vocational training—carpentry, electronics, that sort of thing.

M: In that case we are best off at Enderby Comprehensive. I gather they have excellent workshops and instructors. But it says here that Don well also has good facilities. Enderby High has a little, but they are mostly academic. No vocational training at all at Carlton Abbey or Saint Mary's.

W: What are the schools like academically? How many children go on to university every year?

M: Well, Enderby High is very good — and Carlton Abbey even better, 70% of their pupils go onto university. Donwell isn't so good. Only 8%. And Enderby Comprehensive in Saint Mary's not much more, about 10%.

W: Well, it seems like there is a broad selection of schools. But we have to find out more than statistics before we can decide.

Questions 12 to 15 are based on the conversation you have just heard.

12. What do they want their children to have?

13. What do the speakers say about little Keith?

14. What school has the highest percentage of pupils who go on to university?

15. What are the speakers going to do next?

◇ Section B

- **Passage One**

Good morning, ladies and gentlemen! As instructed in our previous meeting, the subcommittee on building development has now drawn up a brief to submit to the firm's architect. In short, the building would consist of two floors. There would be a storage area in the basement be used by the research center as well as by other departments. We are, as you know, short of storage base, so the availability of a large basement would be a considerable advantage. The ground floor would be occupied by laboratories. Altogether there would be six labs. In addition, there would be six offices for the technicians, plus a general secretarial office and reception area.

The first floor would be occupied by the offices of Research and Development staff. There would be a suite of offices for the Research and Development director as well as a general office for secretarial staff. It's proposed to have a staff room with a small kitchen. This would serve both floors. There would also be a library for research documents and reference materials. In addition, there would be a resource room in which audiovisual equipment and other equipment of that sort could be stored. Finally, there would be a seminar room with closed circuit television. This room could also be used to present displays and demonstrations to visitors to the center. The building would be of brick construction so it's to conform to the general style of construction on the site. There would be a pitched roof. Wall and ceiling spaces would be insulated to conform to new building regulations.

Questions 16 to 18 are based on the passage you have just heard.

16. What is said about the planned basement of the new building?

17. Where would be the Research and Development director's office?

18. Why would the building be of brick construction?

- **Passage Two**

Huang Yi works for a company that sells financial software to small and medium size businesses. His job is to show customers how to use the new software. He spends two weeks with each client, demonstrating the features and functions of the software. The first few months in the job were difficult. He often left the client feeling that even after two weeks he hadn't been able to show the employees everything they needed to know. It's not that they weren't interested; they obviously appreciated his instruction and showed a desire to learn. Huang couldn't figure out if the software was difficult for them to understand, or if he was not doing a good job of teaching. During the next few months, Huang started to see some patterns.

He would get to a new client site and spend the first week going over the software with the employees. He usually did this in shifts, with different groups of employees listening to his lecture. Then he would spend the next week in installing the program and helping individuals troubleshoot. Huang realized that during the week of troubleshooting and answering questions, he ended up addressing the same issues over and over. He was annoyed because most of the individuals with whom he worked seem to have retained very little information from the first week. They asked very basic questions and often needed prompting from beginning to end. At first, he wondered if these people were just a little slow, but then he began to get the distinct feeling that part of the problem might be his style presenting information.

Questions 19 to 22 are based on the passage you have just heard.

19. What does Huang Yi do in his company?

20. What did Huang Yi think of his work?

21. What did Huang Yi do in addition to lecturing?

22. What did Huang Yi realize in the end?

- **Passage Three**

As we help children get out into the world to do their learning well, we can get more of the world into the schools. Aside from their parents, most children never have any close contact with any adults except their teachers. No wonder they have no idea what adult life or work is like. We need to bring more people who are not full-time teachers into the schools. In New York City, under the teachers' and writers' collaborative, real writers come into the schools, read their works, and talk to the children about the problems of their crafts. The children love it. In another school, a practicing attorney comes in every month and talks to several classes about the law. Not the law that is in books, but the law as he sees it and encounters it in his cases. And the children listen with intense interest. Here's something even easier: let children work together, help each other, learn from each other and each other's mistakes. We now know from this experience of many schools that children are often the best teachers of other children.

What's more important, we know that when the fifth floor six-grader who is being having trouble with reading, starts helping a first grader, his own reading sharply improves. A number of schools are beginning to use what some call paired learning. This means that you let children form partnerships with other children. Do their work even including their tests together and share whatever marks or results this work gets. Just like grown-ups in the real world. It seems to work.

Questions 23 to 25 are based on the passage you have just heard.

23. Why does the speaker say most children have no idea what adult life is like?
24. What is happening in New York City schools?
25. What does the experience of many schools show?

◇ Section C

Tests may be the most unpopular part of academic life. Students hate them because they produce fear and anxiety about being evaluated, and focus on grades instead of learning for learning's sake.

But tests are also valuable. A well-constructed test identifies what you know and what you still need to learn. Tests help you see how your performance compares to that of others. And knowing that you'll be tested on a body of material is certainly likely to motivate you to learn the material more thoroughly.

However, there's another reason you might dislike tests: You may assume that tests have the power to define your worth as a person. If you do badly on a test, you may be tempted to believe that you've received some fundamental information about yourself from the professor, information that says you're a failure in some significant way.

This is a dangerous and wrong-headed assumption. If you do badly on a test, it doesn't mean you are a bad person or stupid. Or that you'll never do better again, and that your life is ruined. If you don't do well on a test, you're the same person you were before you took the test — no better, no worse. You just did badly on a test. That's it. In short, tests are not a measure of your value as an individual — they are a measure only of how well and how much you studied. Tests are tools; they are indirect and imperfect measures of what we know.

Appendix B   The Keys

■ Chapter 1

• Compound Dictation One

1. incredible

2. unbelievable performances

3. fierce talent

4. you have forged your way into history these past 2 years

5. collectively

6. climate change is read

7. It is the most urgent threat facing our entire species,

8. big polluters

9. this amazing award tonight

10. take tonight for granted

• Compound Dictation Two

1. images have provoked reactions in people, and those reactions have caused change to happen

2. images that transcend borders, that transcend religions, images that provoke us to step up and do something

3. Images often push us to question our core beliefs and our responsibilities to each other

4. This destructive power takes many different forms

5. images have power to shed light of understanding on suspicion, ignorance

• Cultural Understanding

1. Keys are open

2. Keys are open

References : The foreign cultures, through the medium of their cultural products, are here to invade more and more of our daily life. Faced with such an invasion, some may hold that it will add color and diversity to our national culture, while others argue that it will produce a negative effect on our own culture.

• Cultural Listening Comprehension

1. A   2. B   3. A   4. D   5. A

6. B	7. D	8. C	9. C	10. B
11. A	12. A	13. D	14. C	15. A
16. D	17. C	18. B	19. A	20. D
21. C	22. B	23. B	24. A	25. B

■ Chapter 2

· Compound Dictation One

1. a matter of perspective

2. the combination of incredibly alien vocabulary combined with insanely difficult grammar

3. what is normally called Chinese or Chinese dialects

4. Instead it uses an archaic writing system based on one called ideograms.

5. It takes years and years even as a Chinese person to learn enough of the characters to be literate

6. makes HK Cantonese one of the most difficult languages in the world to learn

7. the intimate clicking sound of language that requires unique precision

8. preserve the secrecy of information and confuse the enemy

9. stresses the way something was done instead of when it was done

10. outwit the Japanese at every turn

11. a verb itself contains virtually all information of the things conveyed in the sentence

· Compound Dictation Two

1. about language loss and the globalization of English

2. how important it is to be able to communicate across generations

3. languages are dying at an unprecedented (前所未有的) rate

4. English is the undisputed (不可置疑的) global language

5. from being a mutually beneficial practice to becoming a massive (大规模的) international business

6. can it be right to reject a student on linguistic ability alone

7. Now it can be dangerous to give too much power to a narrow segment (狭隘的部分) of society. Maybe the barrier would be too universal.

8. If you think about the Islamic Golden Age, there was lots of translation then

9. light shone upon the Dark Ages of Europe

10. I am against using it as a barrier

11. equates (相当于) intelligence with a knowledge of English, which is quite arbitrary

12. hey are prohibitive

13. Education: The Great Divide

14. If you can't think a thought, you are stuck. But if another language can think that thought, then, by cooperating, we can achieve and learn so much more

15. When a language dies, we don't know what we lose with that language

16. the children in his village get the same grades at school as the children who have electricity at home

17. Let us celebrate diversity. Mind your language. Use it to spread great ideas

- **Cultural Understanding**

1. Keys are open

2. Keys are open

- **Cultural Listening Comprehension**

1. A	2. B	3. C	4. D	5. A
6. B	7. B	8. C	9. C	10. D
11. B	12. A	13. D	14. A	15. C
16. A	17. B	18. C	19. D	20. D
21. C	22. D	23. B	24. D	25. A

■ Chapter 3

- **Compound Dictation One**

1. Russia reportedly destroyed 300 tons of food from nations which had imposed sanctions on them

2. in a fairly constant state of tension

3. they are heavily armed and surrounded by technology but weak and ineffectual without it

4. with the buildup of NATO forces throughout Eastern Europe following the collapse of Soviet Union

5. As a direct representation of East meets with the West ideological and political disagreements

6. A mix of historical tension, political rivalry, cultural clash, sanctions and heavy propaganda

7. in exchange for bailing out their tremendous debt

8. the two countries have come head to head

9. deposition

10. near assassination

11. when Hitler invaded Greece in 1941

12. hundreds of thousands dying of hunger or being murdered

13. German soldiers massacred over 200 Greeks in retaliation for

14. paid toughly 6 million Euros as war reparations

15. Greece passionately objected to closing the issue

16. The two countries have intense history that is doing them no favors in calming the waters

· **Compound Dictation Two**

1. the condition and coloration of the bruises
2. It's like roasted beef
3. a traditional Chinese medical treatment
4. I had this on me endless time when I as a kid
5. it's like small streams that run into rivers and then into seas
6. Western mind doesn't understand what you said
7. an authoritative medical expert to make your testimony in plain English
8. Video game design is a collective activity
9. a violent all-powerful monkey
10. a man steep in the culture of violence
11. Sun Wukong (monkey king) is a good-hearted and compassionate hero. He represent our traditional values and ethics
12. A certain fairy creates the pill of eternal youth. Not only is this odd Sun Wukong consuming the entire pills and not leave it for anyone else, but he also overturns the furnace and destroys the workshop that take millennium to construct
13. Gua sha is able to stimulate and increase the volume and flow of blood cells, which is beneficial to the blood circulation
14. You will not consider that abuse, won't you

· **Cultural Understanding**

1. Keys are open
2. Keys are open

· **Cultural Listening Comprehension**

1. B	2. A	3. A	4. C	5. D
6. D	7. B	8. C	9. A	10. B
11. A	12. B	13. D	14. A	15. B
16. B	17. B	18. A	19. D	20. B
21. A	22. C	23. C	24. B	25. A

■ Chapter 4

· **Compound Dictation One**

1. blockbuster
2. He's a genius and also a complete prick

3. tells the world he's decided to be a real life superhero

4. Bruce was a wimpy scientist working with the US government who was tricked into participating in a military experiment that gave him unwanted power

5. When he gets angry or excited, he turns into a big dumb green rage monster

6. Tony became a global superstar as Iron Man

7. He uses a magic hammer that can only be held by those that the hammer deems worthy

8. makes him super strong and they gave him a super power shield

9. they get together and defeated the bad guy during a big fat battle

10. SHIELD is riding high after saving the world and cap is their poster child

11. Cap goes all Ed Snowden on everybody and tells the world about the evil inside SHIELD

• Compound Dictation Two

1. Uncle Sam has to promise to pay interest on these bonds just as you do on any loan you take out

2. It's such a huge amount of money that Uncle Sam is starting to run out of people to borrow from

3. The same goes for the U.S. dollar. The more dollars there are, the less each one will buy

4. to move their factories overseas and pay their workers a few pennies a day too. This contributes to a recession

5. When your dollars are worth less, and you're not earning more of them, that's called stagflation

6. investors, and foreign governments who are counting on that money won't be able to pay their bill

7. If one link in a debt chain stops paying, defaults, the whole thing falls apart

8. If foreign governments can't pay their bills, their own banks and corporations will have the same problems

9. That's called a global economic collapse

• Cultural Understanding

1. Keys are open

2. Keys are open

• Cultural Listening Comprehension

1. D	2. A	3. D	4. B	5. A
6. B	7. C	8. C	9. B	10. A
11. C	12. A	13. D	14. D	15. B
16. D	17. B	18. A	19. C	20. B
21. D	22. D	23. A	24. A	25. C

■ Chapter 5

· Compound Dictation One

1. I'm constantly looking for creative ways to spark challenging conversations

2. the lotus is a symbol for transcendence and for purity of mind and spirit

3. universalize and transcend the history and trauma of black America

4. create a 28-foot version in steel as a permanent installation

5. but people believe these to be imbued with power, or even magic

6. who frequently walk away with no punishment at all

7. I dip them in a thick, brown wax before taking them to a shooting range

8. which bears the marks of its violent creation like battle wounds or scars

9. reminded him that these killings have been going on for over 500 years

10. I hope my artwork creates a safe space for this type of honest exchange

· Compound Dictation Two

1. We were missing the stories about Iraq, the people who live there, and what was happening to them under the weight of the war

2. From conflict zones to climate change to all sorts of issues around crises in public health, we were missing what I call the species-level issues, because as a species, they could actually sink us

3. Just around that time where I was making that observation, I looked across the border of Iraq and noticed there was another story we were missing: the war in Syria

4. And we found it was a model that scaled. We got passionate requests to do other things "Deeply"

5. We have ideas for how to make things better, and I want to share three of them that we've picked up in our own work

6. Like this one from the suburbs of Damascus, about a wheelchair race that gave hope to those wounded in the war

7. But what we saw was a public that was flooded with hysterical and sensational coverage, sometimes inaccurate, sometimes completely wrong

8. It's our job as journalists to get elbow deep in complexity and to find new ways to make it easier for everyone else to understand

· Cultural Understanding

1. Keys are open

2. Keys are open

References: The body language in our daily life is incalculable. Everyone can use his body to represent himself. Body language is the same as verbal language to be the carrier of culture that may cause misunderstanding in the international communication because of culture difference. Having the knowledge of body language will be helpful to us in intercultural communication.

- **Cultural Listening Comprehension**

1. B	2. A	3. B	4. D	5. D
6. C	7. C	8. C	9. B	10. B
11. A	12. C	13. C	14. D	15. A
16. A	17. C	18. C	19. B	20. D
21. C	22. B	23. B	24. A	25. C

■ Chapter 6

- **Compound Dictation One**

1. Each dance has steps that everyone can agree on, but it's about the individual and their creative identity

2. The present always contains the past and the past shapes who we are and who we will be

3. this dance was a way for enslaved Africans to remember where they're from

4. It was about keeping cultural traditions alive and retaining a sense of inner freedom under captivity

5. a way for the enslaved to throw shade at the masters

6. swing dancing

7. had the freedom to kick their heels and move their legs

8. if you knew the steps, it meant you belonged to a group

9. Through social dance, the boundaries between groups become blurred

- **Compound Dictation Two**

1. After their deaths, a bone from each of their skeletons was crafted by human hands into a flute

2. But that is exactly what our ancestors did

3. new ideas come into the world simply because they're fun

4. But in fact, the origins of the modern computer are much more playful, even musical, than you might imagine

5. when a bunch of inventors finally hit on the idea of using a keyboard to trigger not sounds but letters

6. The whole idea of hardware and software becomes thinkable for the first time with this invention

7. why not program it to weave delightful patterns of color out of cloth

8. Paper turned out to be much cheaper and more flexible as a way of programming the device

9. There's a long list of world-changing ideas and technologies that came out of play

10. Now, I think this has implications for how we teach kids in school and how we encourage innovation in our workspaces

- **Cultural Understanding**

1. Keys are open

2. Keys are open

References: Even a little knowledge of the language can make a difference in attitude when you meet people from other countries. Speaking another language helps to break down barriers. It can help you give an added advantage in your career if you work for an international firm or a company with international customers or contacts. If you like literature, films or music from other countries, learning the language will help your appreciation and understanding. You can learn a language in short, bite-sized sessions and you'll enjoy a sense of satisfaction from achieving short-term goals, such as learning how to say hello, introducing yourself or numbers 1–10.

- **Cultural Listening Comprehension**

1. B	2. A	3. D	4. C	5. D
6. B	7. A	8. C	9. D	10. A
11. C	12. B	13. C	14. A	15. B
16. C	17. D	18. A	19. C	20. A
21. C	22. A	23. B	24. C	25. B

■ Chapter 7

- **Compound Dictation One**

1. explain the different meanings of words in Britain and America to help strengthen the union between our two nations

2. a container with a sprout and handle for pouring liquid

3. steam whistles in a factory that signal the cessation of work

4. a silvery white metal

5. With ice-cream

6. a person trained to look after the healthy appearance of your teeth

7. a British airforce missile

8. An annoying man who is on TV in America

9. Sudden death penalty shootout

10. friends or family members leave messages for you to listen to later

11. a fictional boy wizard

12. it's fantasy

- **Compound Dictation Two**

1. like living in the U.S. but with English accents

2. basically completely different

3. it implies that they don't look alright

4. introspection about whether or not I look miserable or not

5. I were trying to buy illicit drugs

6. if you want your complementary shot gun

7. get 30 degree ... a knife that can barely cut a baby carrot

8. have a different concept of what counts as "travel food"

9. there is a somewhere to buy a sandwich

10. even more bizarre is how unfearful English drivers are when they come to pedestrians

11. the strangest thing that I have encountered in the UK is side walk

12. how many times I have been walking down at the left side of the side walk here ..., will slowly drift to the right hand side right directly in front of me

13. all my judgments aside

14. I got a chance to experience them

- **Cultural Understanding**

1. Keys are open

2. Keys are open

- **Cultural Listening Comprehension**

1. D	2. A	3. D	4. C	5. A
6. B	7. D	8. A	9. C	10. B
11. C	12. D	13. D	14. B	15. A
16. D	17. C	18. C	19. D	20. B
21. A	22. B	23. C	24. A	25. B

26. anxiety

27. identifies

28. compares

29. a body of

30. motivate

31. define

32. fundamental

33. ruined

34. In short

35. imperfect

References

[1]　Barna, LaRay M. How Culture Shock Affects Communication. Communication 5.1 (n.d.): 1–18. SocINDEX with Full Text. EBSCO. 29 Sept. 2009. web.

[2]　胡超. 跨文化交际实用教程[M]. 北京: 外语教学与研究出版社，2006.

[3]　James, Paul.Despite the Terrors of Typologies: The Importance of Understanding Categories of Difference and Identity. Interventions: International Journal of Postcolonial Studies. 2015. 17(2): 174-195.

[4]　Kim, Young Yun. Toward an interactive theory of communication-acculturation. Communication Year book. 1979: 3, 435-453.

[5]　Kim, Y. Y.. Development of intercultural identity. Paper presented at the Annual Conference of the International Communication Association, Miami FLA. 1992，05.

[6]　Lauring, Jakob. Intercultural Organizational Communication: The Social Organizing of Interaction in International Encounters. Journal of Business and Communication. 2011.

[7]　Macionis, John, Linda Gerber. Chapter 3-Culture. Sociology. 7th edition ed. Toronto. Pearson Canada Inc., 2010.

[8]　Moha Ennaji. Multilingualism, Cultural Identity, and Education in Morocco. Springer Science & Business Media, 2005.

[9]　Pedersen, Paul. The Five Stages of Culture Shock: Critical Incidents Around the World. Contributions in Psychology. Westport, Conn: Greenwood Press, 1995.

[10]　http://blog.sina.com.cn/s/blog_90df35a00101fqfl.htm.

[11]　http://communication-design.net/3-tips-for-effective-global-communication//Intercultural Communication Law & Legal Definition. Definitions. uslegal.com. Retrieved 2016-05-19.

[12]　https://en.wikipedia.org/wiki/Culture_shock.

[13]　https://en.wikipedia.org/wiki/Hofstede%27s_cultural_dimensions_theory.

[14]　https://plato.stanford.edu/entries/social-norms/.

[15]　http://www.answers.com/Q/How_are_language_and_culture_related.

[16]　https://www.boundless.com/management/textbooks/boundless-management-textbook/introduction-to-management-1/current-challenges-in-management-21/the-challenge-of-globalizat-ion-133-10568/.